Praise for *Witch Hunt*

"Kristen Sollée, author of *Witches, Sluts, Feminists,* explores the archetype of the witch in this entertaining mix of travel guide, journal, and ghost story collection. Highlights include an examination of the divination culture of Italy, including the tarot-dedicated Museo dei Tarocchi in Bologna, and of England's occultism, including the Chelsea Physic Garden in London, where 'the occult is inseparable from the landscape.' Historical figures such as Joan of Arc in France and Dame Alice in Ireland are recast both as early examples of gender-fluidity and powerful women who were killed by fearful men. These and other historic women are featured in fictionalized 'visions' that overcome Sollée, and work as a narrative device in which the dead impart knowledge of their craft and details of their often violent fates. While the author admits these scenes are fantastical, they nicely round out and give context to the catalogue of sites visited."

—*Publishers Weekly*

"Sorceresses of ancient Rome casting love spells with their menstrual blood. Joan of Arc speaking to angels. The cunning women of Ireland and their flying ointments. The witches of Kristen Sollée's new book teach us how to live magically. Impeccably researched and keenly felt—to read this book is to enter into a romance with the witch. A traveler's tryst. Sollée's love of place, the moss and the cobble stones, the ocean spray and the crumbling cemeteries puts her in a polyamorous love affair with the witch and the world in which she lives. This book makes clear that the witch is a creature of her environment. Magic is embodied. The lands through which Sollée travels contain the spirits of the people who collected herbs on their hillsides and spoke their enchantments into the wind. But as with so many love affairs born on holiday, behind all the beauty, the heart grips in grief. We know how the story ends. The witches in this book were hunted after all. But even though we know the story of many of these witches ends in sorrow, we carry on our love affair with them anyway, because to love is to be fully alive. And none are more fully alive than the witch. It's clear that Sollée fell in love with the witches in this book. Sollée's magic is that, if you read it, you will too."

—Amanda Yates Garcia, author of *Initiated: Memoir of a Witch* and host of the Between the Worlds podcast

"There is now a very clear need for a travel guide that deals with places associated with historic and contemporary views of witchscraft; and therefore, it is a real pleasure to find one so extensive, well-written, well-informed, and good humored."

—Ronald Hutton, author of *The Witch: A History of Fear, from Ancient Times to the Present*

WITCH HUNT

A TRAVELER'S GUIDE

WITCH HUNT

TO THE POWER & PERSECUTION

OF THE WITCH

Kristen J. Sollée

WEISER
BOOKS

This edition first published in 2020 by Weiser Books, an imprint of
Red Wheel/Weiser, LLC
With offices at:
65 Parker Street, Suite 7
Newburyport, MA 01950
www.redwheelweiser.com

ISBN: 978-1-57863-699-0
Library of Congress Cataloging-in-Publication Data available upon request.

Cover design by Micol Hiatt
Interior by Kathryn Sky-Peck
Typeset in Adobe Caslon Pro

Printed in the United States of America
LB

10 9 8 7 6 5 4 3 2 1

CONTENTS

ACKNOWLEDGMENTS

Witch Hunt arose from a lifelong immersion in the magic of travel, but only came to fruition because of the support, guidance, and kindness of friends, family, and colleagues. My gratitude goes to Pam Grossman, Micol Hiatt, Sandra Roldan, Kathleen Martens, Bill Sollee, Charlie Schmid, and everyone else who read drafts, contributed ideas, and endeavored to keep me in good spirits along the way. I am grateful to Peter Turner and Weiser Books for giving this book a home and to Christina Oakley Harrington at Treadwell's Books for her invaluable guidance in my research process. I am also indebted to everyone I met on my *Witch Hunt* travels with whom I conversed and communed and gained knowledge about their country's histories. Above all, I offer thanks to my ancestors and those accused of witchcraft in years past. I hope to honor their lives and their deaths with this book.

INTRODUCTION

THE WITCH IS A TRAVELER. She has traversed continents, cultures, and epochs, carrying with her millennia of conflicting ideas about sex and gender, magic and power. The witch has made us travelers, too. She leads us on a journey through the horrors and wonders of myth and history. Seeking the timeless archetypal witch, those who were branded witches centuries ago, and those who identify as witches today requires travel both literal and figurative. *Witch Hunt* is a guide through this mercurial terrain.

Witch Hunt traces the legacy of the witch through significant sites across Europe and North America. Witches no doubt appear in cultures around the world, but the witch who looms largest within the nebulous conceptual region we call the West—the monstrous maiden out to seduce and destroy men, the Satanic sorceress hell-bent on killing crops and livestock, the horrible hag out to consume children—was born in ancient myths, raised in medieval times, and came to full furious fruition in the early modern era.

Between the fifteenth and seventeenth centuries, thousands of people accused of witchcraft suffered and died. Families were ripped apart. Villages were decimated. Terror, torture, and paranoia ravaged communities. It is a delicate matter to craft a travel guide through such horrifying episodes in human history. Whenever we immerse ourselves in periods of historical oppression, we run the risk of glamorizing or aestheticizing them, which can make light of real people's pain and trauma. First and foremost, this book aims to honor the victims of the witch hunts.

And yet, the morbid appeal of the witch hunts is the reason they continue to survive as a subject of intrigue. Cunning women, stunning sirens, and vengeful crones strike fear into the hearts of young and old. Sexually gratuitous confessions and untrammeled cruelty against a backdrop of apocalyptic weather, religious corruption, and personal power struggles; magic, destruction, and seduction all wrapped up with a poisonously pretty bow—the whole thing is so Shakespearean the witch hunts literally inspired the writing of *Macbeth*.

The most curious piece of this puzzle, however, is how we got from *witch* being a word you didn't whisper without fear of recourse in early modern times to an identity voiced proudly by thousands of people in the twenty-first century. "The transformation of the witch from a figure who had occasioned fear and loathing for the best part of 2,000 years into one perceived as sympathetic—even aspirational—is one of the most radical and unexpected developments of modern Western culture," proclaims John Callow in *Embracing the Darkness: A Cultural History of Witchcraft*.

Witch Hunt explores this radical shift in Italy, France, Germany, Ireland, the United Kingdom, and the United States. It tells the story of the witch on the ground, through sight, touch, scent, and sound. My journey began with a visceral need not merely to read history but to feel it in full-body immersion. I sought out art, literature, scripture, and academic scholarship, but my research deepened in the moments when I put myself in a hallowed place and simply sat still. There is no substitute for the magic of place.

The witch is both hexer and healer, the demonic and divine feminine, a malicious spellcaster and an innocent victim of circumstance. She is literary and literal: a figment of the imagination and a figure as real as you or I. "She is a creature of accretion," Pam Grossman writes in *Waking the Witch: Reflections on Women, Magic, and Power*.

The Wicked Witch of the Western World can be traced back to benevolent and brutal mother goddesses as well as female demons like the Mesopotamian *lilitu*, where Jewish lore for Adam's first wife-cum-child-eating-succubus Lilith likely originated. After Lilith refused to submit to Adam and screeched off into the night, her fertile crescent became the breeding ground for countless other demons and evil spirits. She would transform into "one of the great imagined figures of the Western world," Ronald Hutton asserts in *The Witch: A History of Fear, from Ancient Times to the Present*, morphing to become the matriarch of witches to many Europeans during the witch hunts, and an anti-patriarchal radical to many feminists and witchcraft practitioners today.

Another important ancient figure in witch history is Eve. Her transgressive desire for knowledge proffered by Satan's serpentine steward got her and Adam kicked out of paradise, forever branding women in Christian mythology as the untrustworthy cause of man's downfall. Eve's actions in this origin story have had a profound impact on Christian conceptions of gender over the past millennium.

The history of the witch is by no means linear. There are stops and starts and strange detours along the way. Although "ancient traditions played an important role in the formation of European witchcraft beliefs," Hutton writes, they did so in "complicated and subtle ways, and over a long period of time." There is a wealth of scholarly and popular writing on the witch's backstory, but the two foremothers who will arise again and again in this book are Lilith and Eve.

It's no coincidence that these two witchy progenitors are women. In myth and in history, witches do challenge and even transcend binary gender roles, but remain closely associated with women and femininity. About 70–80 percent of the thousands accused of witchcraft and

80–85 percent of those executed for witchcraft were women, so to call the archetypal witch "she" is both historically accurate and, in a way, an honorific. There were many men accused of and executed for witchcraft, however, so gender bias and misogyny alone do not account for the early modern witch hunts.

In the twentieth century, the word *witch* took on new meanings with the birth of modern witchcraft. Those who take part in the diverse nature-based practices that fall under the witchcraft umbrella come in all genders, but many witches on the feminine spectrum feel a special kinship with the witch figure based on a shared experience of sex- and gender-based prejudice and persecution. This kinship is also why some feminists, regardless of spiritual practice, have taken up the witch as an icon in their activism.

For many modern witches, their politics are inseparable from their craft. As new forms of public and private rituals of protest—of civic-minded magic—take shape, analytical discourse is confronting embodied spiritual practice. Rituals of collective hexing and healing are making headlines. Covens are canvassing for political campaigns. Protests are rife with witch-centric messaging. The magical world and the materialist world are melding and in the process catalyzing and fleshing out new ways that politics and spirituality interface in the twenty-first century.

The witch hunts remain deeply misunderstood in the United States, partly because of their continued use as a misappropriated rhetorical device. As John Demos observes in *The Enemy Within: A Short History of Witch-Hunting*, the witch hunt as metaphor is "a mode (most often) of moral reproach." You'll find the phrase applied when there appears to be "some allegation of subversive intent, of conspiratorial menace, of concealed betrayal." But although the historical witch hunts were riddled with subversive intent, it was usually society's most powerful who conspired to betray the most vulnerable. That is why contemporary cries of "witch hunt" from powerful politicians always devolve into ahistoricism. It is therefore vital that we raise awareness about what happened during *real* witch hunts.

Without sacrificing historicity, I decided to dip into the realm of historical fiction at opportune moments to reflect the witch as both a real and imagined figure. Throughout this book, you'll encounter characters from the past constructed from records and fleeting references. They come in animal and human form. "Guilty" and innocent, they put a face to the abstractions of atrocity and make history come alive. As I visited many of the sites where accused witches suffered and died, I did what we all do when we travel to historical sites of any sort: imagine who or what came before.

The irony of writing a book like this today isn't lost on me. As a childless woman on the wrong side of thirty, as a woman with an outspoken distaste for the abuses of patriarchy, as a heathen who has left the Christian fold, I would not have made it very far traveling through most European townships and American cities of yore. But in the twenty-first century, arms adorned with indelible protection sigils, dressed and looking like something Dante would surely envision as one of the Devil's handmaidens, I can still move through the world *mostly* unharmed because of my race and class—apart from the safety concerns that all women traveling alone must face.

Over the past few years, my *Witch Hunt* research brought me to seven countries and forty-five cities, towns, and villages. I stayed at witch-themed hotels, watched witch-centric plays, attended one witchy amusement park and a seaside witch parade, visited two more-than-500-year-old oak trees, partook in a ghost hunt, and perused countless occult bookstores and witch shops. But in a way, I have unwittingly been doing research for this book for far longer.

As an only child of divorce with parents who lived and loved in different parts of the country, I was often alone or traveling alone to visit them. Being shy and introverted, I wasn't interested in people during these times of solitude as much as I was taken with *places* and *things*. Through this animistic approach, I came to view my surroundings as friends, as sources of energy, as entities in themselves that I could get to know, slowly, cautiously, if they opened themselves up to me. Driven by a desire to pick up pieces of the past, and to commune with forests and parks, ancient cities and sacred landmarks, I intuitively engaged with concepts like psychogeography and geomantic empathy before I knew there were names for the ways we can become intimate with the physical and metaphysical aspects of a place and how that place can impact our emotional state.

At three, I was hypnotized by the echoing halls of the Galleria dell'Accademia in Florence and Michelangelo's *David*, the marble "boy with no clothes": who was he, *why* was he, and how did he get there? At ten, I was taken by the dangerous curves of the Minangkabau roofs in Bukittinggi, where my mother and I met women of a Sumatran matrilineal line as they surveyed their coming clove harvest. At eleven, I played with prehistoric lizards that lolled on uninhabited islands around the Great Barrier Reef, and my father and I fed them spiced salami from a picnic basket. At twenty-five, I roamed the shimmering forest around the Ise Grand Shrine alone to pay my respects to the Shinto sun goddess Amaterasu. These experiences are a privilege I acknowledge with gratitude, as they shaped me in ways that are only recently becoming clear.

At first, *Witch Hunt* was driven by this need to connect with the power of place and my intellectual interest in the early modern witch hunts. But as I dug deeper into the research, my own bloodline beckoned. On the DNA ancestry site 23 and Me, a map of progressively darker blues denoting recent genetic inheritance tracked my travels with eerie accuracy—a fact I discovered only after tickets had been bought and itineraries made.

My relatives lived where we know witch hunts once occurred: in London, Lancashire, and Edinburgh. Fainter blues suggest they lived in Bamberg, too. There are even Italian and French lines further back, denoted in murky percentages that don't make the map. I know from my family's research that the Sollée name stretches to Normandy, to people who lived in Rouen, where Joan of Arc burned and witch hunts raged long after that.

It's easy to get swept up in the romance of ancestral imaginings, but in so many magical practices and major religions—in sacred, profane, and everyday ways—we honor our ancestors: relishing opportunities they only dreamed to have, finishing work they only dared to start. Whether we reject or revere our ancestors and their lives, they are an intimate part of who and how we are. Our narratives don't begin with us. We are the climaxes and codas of someone else's story.

Centuries later, the stories of the early modern witch hunts remain meaningful. For some, they are spiritually significant. For others, the witch hunts carry political or ancestral weight. Vital to this legacy are places across Europe and North America that saw the power and the persecution of the witch unfold. *Witch Hunt* is a gateway to these history-haunted cities and sites and a catalyst for the curious venture I call "witch travel."

BLOOD *STREGONERIA*, SEX MAGIC

Florence, Italy

SOMETIMES, THE PAST IS PALPABLE. Tendrils of memory push through in unexpected ways, twisting the veil of time. Oblivious people traipse by, unaware of the stories that played out beneath their feet. Despite the revisions of progress that transform local terrain, we're left with a magical palimpsest in places where the unspeakable occurred. Sometimes a monument or a map marks the spot; other times, it's a feeling you can't shake, forcing you to flip through your guidebook or interrogate the locals, desperate for clues. Sometimes a place all but screams *something happened here*.

This feeling floats like a fog across the center of old Florence. A city known for its taste—renowned art and architecture exalting the glory of God, gustatory pleasures tempting even the most avowed ascetic—it's also a city where history has been written and rewritten, compressing the most marginal voices into a howling din. Apathy threatens to silence them, but if you open yourself up to it, they're there. You might even feel the pull of the place or its protective spirit, what the Romans called *genius loci*. It penetrates your pores.

On my fourth visit to Tuscany, I wasn't content to simply slap on a tourist grin, look at leather shops, at Renaissance art, at locals sharing an after-work carafe under the terra-cotta roofs that shelter the city. I wanted to get at what lies beneath.

Many travel guides prefer to gloss over the grim memories of a place, as if travel were meant only to offer an idyllic version of life to distract from the flaws in your own. But my purpose is to uncover something with a bit more grit and depth so we might venture into the shadows—subterranean travel for a psychogeographic trip.

I arrived in Florence in the middle of a heat wave. Tourists in the streets numbed themselves with gelato and cold white wine, crafting makeshift fans out of street maps and travel brochures. I spent my first few days avoiding the swelter by hiding out in my Airbnb, mere steps from the Museo Galileo, the Arno River, and the Uffizi Gallery. Tucked away inside the Piazza dei Giudici, I sprawled out reading in what was once part of a medieval castle, the stone walls staying relatively cool despite the heat. Knowing I couldn't stay ensconced there forever, I decided to take a long, slow walk on a scorching afternoon.

Visitors waiting to buy tickets for the Uffizi, hungry to feast their eyes on the fearsome and flirty femmes inside—Botticelli's *The Birth of Venus*, Caravaggio's *Medusa*—scattered in serpentine lines across cobblestones of the Piazza della Signoria where Florentines once took in spectacles of a different sort. Now, the square is a panorama of sculptures and cafés and breathtaking buildings. But for centuries, it was the seat of the republic and an abattoir for sin. Before the bonfires of the vanities, when Dominican friar Girolamo Savonarola burned books and instruments and paintings and every possible object tempting to body and soul, women were blamed for inciting similar temptations. These women were "witches" like Giovanna, who, according to city records from 1427, was accused of drawing "the chaste spirit" of a man "for carnal purposes by means of the black arts."

The temperature rose to 101 degrees that day, and I kept walking, wilting, past Santa Croce, past Casa Buonarroti, wandering northeast to the point of delirium. That's when I first saw her, in reflections of my own bleached blonde hair in shop windows: *pasticceria*, *salumeria*, an unending parade of shoes and jackets and purses peering back at me. She was a mirage in every mirrored surface, her green *gammura* kissing the cobblestones, hair in a feral cascade, rouged cheeks raised in a sly smile. Somehow, not a single bead of sweat marred her diaphanous face.

I leaned in to follow the figure's undulations. I was in Sant'Ambrogio now, an area loved for being slightly less of a tourist trap. Weaving my way through the Jewish neighborhood and bustling market stalls, I was in this haunting vision's thrall. Finally, I passed through the great wooden doors of the church of Sant'Ambrogio, and under the vaulted ceilings the apparition took shape. She materialized as Giovanna, born to Francesco El Toso, a woman alive only as much as heat-induced hallucinations allowed her to be.

The air inside the church was thick and still. This was Giovanna's parish, the place Saint Ambrose was once said to have laid down his head in the fourth century. This was a destination of pilgrimages, the foundation unchanged since 1230 when a priest found a chalice of wine had miraculously turned to blood overnight (a fitting place for a practitioner of blood magic to guide me). I sat down on a pew to catch my breath and Giovanna sat—then knelt—next to me, her prayers not supplications, but whispers that pricked my ears. Candle flames did not waver; footsteps did not echo as she shared herself with me.

"Jacopo," she intoned. The stained glass flickered and became a filmstrip of their history. The room filled with their heat; the potency of illicit lust frothed from the corners of her mouth. Jacopo di Andrea was her lover. They had several trysts she tried to extend without luck. She once had him drink her menstrual flow in his wine, afterward chanting, "I will catch you in my net if you don't flee." She made him taste her juices mid-coitus and used enchanted words to seal the spell. Jacopo the doublet maker was hers again and again—until he wasn't.

One look at Giovanna, and you wouldn't think she'd need to use love magic at all. A coquette with a cause, the fine pearls she wore clutched her delicate neck for dear life, in defiance of her adulterous bent. On her, the necklace didn't symbolize innocence. Chastity, humility, virginity: all false gods to a woman who survived on her wits, her wantonness, and, yes, perhaps even her witchcraft. But vanity? Vanity was something she could work with, too.

Using alchemy of a different sort, Giovanna had spent painstaking hours to transform her hair to gold, as was the Florentine fashion. First, taking the shells of walnuts and bark from the same tree, she had boiled them in water, then applied the mixture to her hair, adding alum and apples and tying her tresses up away from her face so it might set. Days later, she added crocus, dragon's blood, henna, and brazilwood to achieve a color cut from the rays of the morning sun, just as the *Trotula* had taught her mother, her grandmother, and her grandmother's mother before her.

Beyond Giovanna's glamour spells, I wanted to know why she had done what she'd done—if she'd done anything at all. *"Da che tu vuo' saver cotanto a dentro, dirotti brievemente."* Her voice hypnotic, like a swarm of bees, she replied with innuendo delivered from Dante. "Since you wish to know so deeply, I will tell you in brief." Hands a steeple, head bowed, she continued to channel her acts of love so I might understand.

After Jacopo came Niccolo, she said, whose children she bore and whom she tried to get back from Hungary and into her arms. That attempt would have her accused of raising a demon in an act of divination and creating wax images for her magic. Giovanna's lips moved rapidly in retelling as her tongue continued to conjure. She spoke of another married man, Giovanni, who paused by her door one day in her parish and couldn't help but stare. His eyes devoured her before she even had the chance to return his gaze, to invite him inside. But she wanted his devotion—and his virility—so Giovanna fashioned a charm out of melted lead that she sweetened with her words. It was from Monna Gilia, the druggist, that she purchased these items.

Giovanna's charms eventually worked—whether magically or metaphorically, I could not be sure. Giovanni was so taken with Giovanna that "his chaste spirit was deflected to lust after her, so that willy-nilly he went several times to her house and there he fulfilled her perfidious desire," the records said. And that might have been the end of the tale. After all, not all adults engaged in adultery make the history books.

But when Giovanni's love did not bloom as brightly as she wanted, she upped the ante. At the advice of a certain priest, she added distilled water from the skulls of dead men to Giovanni's wine. He drank, unwittingly, but it was not enough. Next, she snuck her menstrual blood into Giovanni's cup as she had done with the others, so her paramour could keep up with her carnal demands. And he did for a while. Giovanna reaped her reward and married Giovanni, but as he had betrayed his first wife, he would betray her, too. She knew how it would end—the olive leaves had told her so.

Named a "magician, witch, and sorceress, and a practitioner of the black arts" by the Florentine court, Giovanna left the world littered with the unworthy men she had lured into her bed, all before quite literally losing her head. In early June, she confessed to her crimes—because they were true or because she had no choice. She was beheaded in the square, killed for her desires—or his desires, their desires. In the dim church, in her eyes and on her lips, I did not know which.

Giovanna spoke no more. I left Sant'Ambrogio as merchants flagged me down to inspect scarves and gold rosaries that shimmered in the afternoon light. Driven to see what witchcraft might mean in

Florence of 2019, I crossed over the Ponte Vecchio and took a sharp left on the Via de' Bardi. A pointed witch's hat on a green sign beckoned: La Strega Nocciola.

I remembered it from the first time I visited Florence over a decade before, when I had been told ominously by a local that the women behind the counter knew exactly what flavors would please my palate. This "gelato witch" myth turned out to be partially true, but, much like Giovanna's workings, you're likely to end up with something pleasing when you're dealing with the sweeter things in life like sex or ice cream—even if your magic is a little off.

After my dessert divinations were complete, I licked the last of it from my lips—hazelnut, if you must know—before forging ahead. Past the parks that flanked either side of the street I walked. Past churches and apartment buildings, I was directed by my GPS to stop once I reached a small storefront with an owl in the window, wings outstretched, welcoming. Not dissimilar to the many witch shops I frequent in the United States, La Soffitta delle Streghe smelled of herbs, incense, and melting wax inside. The woman behind the counter began to offer her help through a patchwork of English and Italian, showing off tarot decks and books for sale, as well as divination and healing services.

La Soffitta delle Streghe might seem, for all intents and purposes, the contemporary equivalent of a shop a medieval spellcaster like Giovanna might visit for guidance and the right raw materials. In the recorded details of Giovanna's case, she spoke of consulting two women who helped her in crafting the spellwork necessary to gain the favor of men. There was a "druggist" and a certain "diabolical woman" who came to her aid when she sought their advice.

The druggist's name was revealed, but the second woman's was not "for the public good"—in the event that anyone in possession of the information might attempt Giovanna's spells, too. But the guidance and goods Giovanna required weren't combined into a one-stop shop as they are today. She got her magical needs met where many of her time would: at church, at the apothecary, and from other women in her community.

I perused the selection of books in La Soffitta delle Streghe hoping to learn more about Giovanna's witchcraft. There were volumes on disparate topics like Norse runes, Haitian Voodoo, Eastern mysticism, British Wicca, and contemporary Italian *stregheria*. I kept looking for something distinctive to the area that would help me connect in some way to medieval *stregoneria*. But that, I knew, was a fool's errand.

The Pagan-cum-Catholic folk practices the Florentines deemed witchcraft are largely distinct from most kinds of witchcraft practiced today—and often at odds with the mores of contemporary culture, particularly when it comes to consent in love magic. Although there are certainly surviving grimoires of learned men from medieval and early modern times, the magic of women is harder to uncover. Giovanna's love magic is known more through its persecution than its execution. Her witchcraft lives on in a liminal space.

I left the witch shop with Giovanna's confession in mind, the sun igniting the aquamarine waters of the Arno behind me. Some six hundred years later, the *other woman* archetype lives on. She is the scapegoat, punished for inciting male lust, ruining relationships, and defiling healthy desire, while men often retain their innocence, their victimhood—as Giovanni, Niccolo, and Jacopo likely did. The righteous masses of today still want to watch the other woman metaphorically beaten, broken, and disposed of, much like the bodies of supposed sorceresses in the past—their heads cut off in the piazza, tossed to the crowds, put on pikes for display, or burned beyond recognition as the community watched.

Crossing over the bridge again I found myself back in the Piazza della Signoria. The Uffizi was closed, the tourists scattering back toward their hotels before embarking on dinner excursions. This very square shared the same four corners with the place where women who lusted, cheated, and wanted were assigned the capacity for extraordinary evil and paid with their lives. Head tilting back, I looked up at the rainbow sherbet sky, still holding a little paper bag from the witch shop filled with a Visconti tarot deck and a box of free incense. *"Streghe"* was emblazoned in large black letters across the front. An innocuous enough word now, no one gave it a second glance.

As I began to snap photos of the rather exquisite sunset like dozens of tourists around me, it was tempting to slip back into unknowing. To look at only the beauty the city wanted me to see, to live fully in fantasy. But turning to catch the light just right, I caught Medusa's dead eyes, her severed head hanging from Perseus's hand. Gazing at Benvenuto Cellini's famed bronze statue of a woman who had survived rape only to die a monster, I knew I could not be blissful in ignorance again. Once more, Giovanna's specter rose to greet me. We left the square together to become part of the city night, I, swinging my *"Streghe"* bag, she trailing just at my heels in a fragrant snake of smoke.

There is no one who is not afraid of spells.

—Pliny the Elder

Perceptions of the Italian witch have danced between derision and devotion over the past millennium. Although people on the peninsula did not partake in the persecution of witches to the extent other Europeans did, witches and witchcraft are a vital part of Italian folklore and history. Today, Venice rings in the Epiphany with men in witch drag racing across the Grand Canal to honor La Befana, the temperamental crone said to have aided the three wise men traveling to meet a just-born Jesus. A 600-year-old tree in Capannori called "the Oak of the Witches" has been deemed a national monument because of the legends it has inspired. Genoa teaches its children about malefic *maga* of the past in a yearly ghost hunt that precedes the midnight bonfire on the Feast of San Giovanni. Triora has transformed into a Mediterranean Salem, dedicated to remembering its destructive witch hunt while keeping Pagan practices alive. And listen long enough in any Italian town and you might overhear a superstition about witches that someone's mother or grandmother once told them. (If your leave your clothes on the clothesline overnight, a cab driver cautioned in Sanremo, a witch might enchant them.)

In my search for the Italian witch, I began by peering into the ancient past to find what magical women might be waiting for me there. Sorceresses played significant roles in ancient Mesopotamia and Greece, but what were such women like in ancient Rome?

As Maxwell Teitel Paule explains in *Canidia, Rome's First Witch*: "the Roman witch was persistently conceived of as a malleable and polyvalent entity, not unlike a demon." There's a bounty of words for witch in Latin compared to our limited vocabulary. There's the *praecantrix* (diviner) and the *venefica* (potion maker) as well as the *maga* (what Giovanna was called in Florentine records), the *malefica, saga, lamia, striga*, and even the *quaedam anus*, which just means "some old woman." All these titles refer to "a female in possession of vaguely defined supernatural abilities—and beyond," Paule writes.

In the West, witches have historically been people whose practices conflict with dominant religious dogma. Roman witches were no different. Conceptions of these magical practitioners can be culled from surviving fiction and nonfiction alike. Virgil's *Eclogues* offers one of the earliest uses of the phrase "magic rites" in Latin literature, which the poet links to wicked witch-seductress Circe of Homer's *Odyssey*. Horace's *Satires* parodies the sensuous Circe through the character

Canidia, a hideous crone who casts her own kind of vengeful, erotic spells. Lucan's Thessalian witch Erictho from *Pharsalia* (and, much later, Dante's *Inferno* and Goethe's *Faust*) is yet another horrible hag who gets up to necromantic no good.

Ancient Roman perspectives on magic shifted gradually over time. In the first century AD, Pliny the Elder deemed magic the "most fraudulent of the arts" in a particularly brutal takedown in *Natural History*, disparaging lowly foreigners in Persia and Britain who indulged in it. Aligning with Pliny, Roman law became increasingly hostile to those who trafficked in charms, potions, and spells. By the second century AD, the idea of *magia* (magic) had converged with *maleficium* (crime/ evil deed).

Derek Collins notes in *Magic in the Ancient Greek World* that "by late antiquity an explicitly criminal coloring was given to all activities that could be squeezed into a definition of 'magic.'" Ancient Rome would further influence medieval and early modern witchcraft beliefs when the empire began to Christianize in the fourth century. This is when the term *Pagan* begins to pop up with some frequency to delineate (and denigrate) non-Christians. Though the word is now embraced by many witches, *Pagan* was not a term that polytheists of the ancient world used to describe themselves. The very idea of Paganism flattens countless complex practices and belief systems and was solely the invention of early Christians, James J. O'Donnell explains in *Pagans: The End of Traditional Religion and the Rise of Christianity*. And just as the term *Pagan* was entering the mainstream, Roman theologian Augustine of Hippo came along and began to flesh out the Christian pantheon of evil.

"Augustine would make it clear that the gods of old were nothing more and nothing less than the fallen angels of the Old Testament," O'Donnell writes, "and he and his coreligionists used a good old word for them: *demons*." Saint Augustine also proposed that a pact with a demon was what gave spellcasters their power. And what was the most common kind of demon-driven magic ancient Romans indulged in at the time? Love magic.

Binding love magic—what the Florentine sorceress Giovanna was accused of wielding—dates back centuries before her time. And it was just as likely to get you in trouble with the law. Apuleius, a Platonist philosopher, poet, and magician of some renown, was accused of using love magic to get his much older and wealthier wife to marry him in AD 159. ("Love magic," Brian Copenhaver explains in *The Book of Magic: From Antiquity to the Enlightenment*, "was on sale everywhere" in ancient Rome.) At his trial, Apuleius defended himself using clever rhetoric about the origins and nature of magic itself. His defense is actually the first recorded instance of the phrase *magica maleficia* (maleficent magic) in Roman literature. Because of this, Derek Collins posits that "the long history of *maleficium* as 'maleficent magic' and, later, 'witchcraft' begins with Apuleius."

Fast-forward a thousand years or so and love magic was still pervasive—and prohibited—by the time Giovanna was getting hot and heavy. Popular ingredients in Italian love spells of her day could range from holy oil and wax images or figures to animal hearts, semen, pubic hair, and human blood. "Blood is thick with magical significations, mystical claims, pharmacological prodigies, [and] alchemistic dreams," Piero Camporesi rhapsodizes in *Juice of Life: The Symbolic and Magic Significance of Blood*.

Giovanna was merely following convention when she served her intimate liquids to Jacopo and Giovanni without their knowledge or consent. The use of menstrual blood in binding love magic "was a uniquely powerful sign of a woman's fertility and thus highly suitable," asserts Guido Ruggiero in *Binding Passions: Tales of Magic, Marriage, and Power at the End of the Renaissance*. Mixing menstrual blood secretly into wine and offering it to a man to make him yours was de rigueur.

Love magic flourished in Florence and beyond in the late medieval and early modern period. It was the most common kind of witchcraft the Inquisition saw in sixteenth-century Modena—and was found all over Siena, Rome, and Venice, too. Ruggiero affirms there was "a highly articulated discourse concerned with magical power over love that was widely understood and practiced in late-sixteenth-century Venice, and that it was dominated by women and women's networks."

When love magic facilitated a match that was socially agreeable, no one usually had cause to complain. But when "matches were seen as incorrect, crossing class lines, thwarting the wishes of the powerful, or even merely creating unhappy marriages, the same magic could quickly become evil in the eyes of the community and was much more likely to come to the attention of the authorities," Ruggiero writes.

Love magic was risky business. But then, again, love in medieval and early modern times was a different animal.

As Maria Helena Sanchez Ortega explains of love magicians in the Middle Ages, "these enamored women were not satisfied merely with having their love reciprocated." Reading between the lines of Giovanna's court records reveals that she was probably out for more, too.

"Their aspirations and amorous passion extended to the total control of the beloved's will," Ortega writes in "Sorcery and Eroticism in Love Magic." "Our enamored women, practitioners of magic, were essentially pragmatic souls who realized that they must obtain masculine support at all costs, so as not to be socially devalued. Yet the purely amorous or erotic aspect of most of these practices is undeniable."

Throughout my travels across the winding backstreets of Florence, I thought of Giovanna and her ilk often. At a time when there were no dating apps, and respectable women could not carouse freely in public places or be sexual or romantic aggressors, love magic ruled the day. Florence is still considered one of the most romantic cities in the world, and lovers from all over leave locks across the Arno as rites of commitment. Who among us hasn't engaged in some kind of spellcraft or magical thinking when it comes to love?

Practitioners of love magic acted in ways that don't always square with our vision of witchcraft today. Many discussions of the historical witch only highlight her victimhood. The women executed for witchcraft were indeed victims of a patriarchal religion and a patriarchal state, but there were those—like the love magicians described above—who happened to actively partake in the "crimes" or practices they were charged with. Acting in accordance with their needs until the moment their lives were taken, these women lusted for sexual partners, powerful marriages, and the soft embrace of love, and they used what they had at their disposal to get it. In that sense, these real-life love witches weren't victims, but agents of desire. Their stories have played out in blood and in wine, in apothecaries, churches, and bedrooms since ancient times.

DIVINATION NATION

Florence and Bologna, Italy

The first art that the demon ever created was that of divination . . .
thus he said on earth to Lady Eve: eat of this fruit and you
will know good and evil and will be gods.

—BERNARDINO OF SIENA

A MONTH BEFORE I LEFT FOR ITALY, a curious email appeared in my inbox. Purple astrological emojis dotted the subject line: my "travel horoscope" awaited inside. "Look to the stars for travel inspiration," *Reservations.com* instructed, leading me to click on my Sun sign (Capricorn) to "reveal where you should travel next and why." Although I prefer to choose my destinations through more material means (spinning a globe, naturally), the tactic had my attention. Leveraging the public's passion for astrology is something organizations both sacred and profane have been doing for a very long time.

Love it, hate it, or live and die by it—astrology is a significant part of contemporary culture—and witchcraft. Wiccans, neo-Pagans, eclectic witches, and magical dilettantes alike armor up for retrogrades, celebrate eclipses, and chart their personal and professional lives through the solar system's vicissitudes. You don't have to be a witch to be into astrology, but most witches are in deep. It's no coincidence that with the witchcraft revival in full swing, astrological devotion has increased exponentially in the mainstream.

"Millennials have replaced religion with astrology," declared a 2019 piece in the *LA Times*. And the oft-maligned millennial is more than likely to have used an astrology app, shared a star sign meme, or paid for a scathing birth chart read. In many circles, the idea of self-care has become as much about caring for your physical body as it is understanding the impact that heavenly bodies have on it. Astrology is seemingly inescapable right now, much to the delight of devotees and the chagrin of debunkers.

The sun was still blazing the day I went hunting for Florentine astrology. Crossing the Arno from the comfort of my medieval stone apartment, I steadily climbed hundreds of steps up to a religious complex known for a divinatory treasure. The heat threatened to spike that afternoon, so I pushed on despite feeling faint, the green and white marble of San Miniato al Monte seemingly a mirage in the distance.

Built between the eleventh and thirteenth centuries on the foundation of a far older shrine to Saint Minias, San Miniato al Monte is a breathtaking specimen of Tuscan Romanesque architecture situated on one of the highest points in the city. If you want to take in vistas of Florence, this is the place. Pilgrims of all sorts make the trek daily for San Miniato's views and to see one of its not-so-secret features: a marble zodiac mosaic on the church floor featuring twelve astrological symbols.

Designed to track the passage of time and to mark important Christian feasts, San Miniato al Monte's basilica is positioned in such a way that sunbeams enter and illuminate different parts of the church—and the zodiac—as the year goes by. Stepping into the cavernous basilica, I found the zodiac panel in the center aisle surrounded by protective ropes. The intricacy is astounding in this well-preserved artifact: I initially made out the shape of a bull, a goat, two fish, and a crab amid decorative filigree. During the Feast of San Giovanni (which is also the summer solstice), light rushes in to electrify the symbol of the crab set into a circle for Cancer season. This zodiac inlay remains the oldest working solstice meridian in all of Europe, but was likely inspired by an even older zodiac inside another building of green and white marble: the Baptistery of San Giovanni.

An octagonal minor basilica across from the Duomo, the Baptistery was consecrated in the eleventh century. Some scholars believe its zodiac panel was installed so light would shine through the Baptistery and alight on the symbol of the sun to mark the Feast of San Giovanni. The zodiac was repositioned centuries ago, however, so it unfortunately no longer serves its original purpose—although it is still there to visit. Touring the Baptistery didn't make much sense until I saw San Miniato. Nearly identical in both form and function, the two marble zodiac panels are companion pieces that tell us much about astrology of the past.

While pondering these Pagan-cum-Christian marvels, I ventured next door to the basilica where members of the Olivetan order were serving homemade ice cream, a welcome antidote for the heat. Inside the San Miniato gift shop, I perused handcrafted oils for calming your anxiety and vivifying your skin in addition to all sorts of wares picturing the zodiac panel, from silk scarves to gold jewelry. A monk pointed out a necklace with a Cancerian crab on it, and I began to wonder whether the pope would approve of all this astrological idolatry.

"All forms of divination are to be rejected," the Catechism of the Catholic Church decrees. "Consulting horoscopes, astrology, palm reading, interpretation of omens and lots, the phenomena of clairvoyance, and recourse to mediums . . . contradict the honor, respect, and loving fear that we owe to God alone." There seems to be no place for astrology in today's Catholicism—let alone any form of divination—but there has always been a lag between what is practiced and what is preached.

Italy has long been a nation of divination. "Divination was built into Rome's culture, politics, and military prowess," explains Brian Copenhaver, "not just its religion." It was common for citizens and officials alike to consult with fortune-tellers, dream interpreters, and astrologers. Roman astrology drew on practices that began in ancient Mesopotamia and developed further in Greece. Studying celestial bodies and interpreting the stars and planets' impact on people and events were not viewed as separate disciplines as they are now: the line between astronomy and astrology was blurry at best.

There were ancient Romans who famously questioned the validity of astrology—Pliny the Elder, for one—but the stars had the last laugh. Astrology was eventually "integrated into the Roman canon of sciences, as one of the seven *artes*," writes Kocku von Stuckrad in *History of Western Astrology*, and "the 'language of the stars' became a kind of lingua franca, in which various cultural areas and religious traditions could easily communicate."

So how did zodiac symbols find their way into Christian churches like San Miniato al Monte and the Baptistery of San Giovanni? You might think once Christianity began to draw a following that astrology was shown the door, but the opposite occurred. In fact, in the early Christian era, astrology "became the main discipline for interpreting the world and the future," von Stuckrad explains. But it had to be integrated into the new religion first.

Overwriting astrology's Pagan past, newly minted Christians began to shift the meanings of the zodiac. The twelve signs came to symbolize Jesus's twelve apostles. The Sun came to symbolize Christ himself, who was worshipped on Sunday. It took centuries to Christianize the zodiac, but convert Saint Zeno of Verona proffered in-depth links between Christian theology and astrology in the fourth century AD.

Contemporary astronomer Simone Bartolini, who has worked extensively at San Miniato and the Baptistery, details the zodiac's early

Christianized meanings in *Sun and Symbols: The Zodiacs in the Basilica of San Miniato al Monte and in the Baptistry of San Giovanni in Florence*:

> According to [Saint Zeno's] interpretation, Aries became the symbol of the mystic Lamb that would be sacrificed; Taurus represented Christ's sacrifice and the divine drama, while Cancer and Leo represented the resurrection and the triumph of Light. Gemini is the symbol of the transition from the Old to the New Testament through the mystical womb of Mary, represented by the sign of Virgo. The remaining signs of the zodiac symbolized human drama, based on the passage from human ruin and perdition to redemption by Christ's sacrifice, here represented in the highest expression in Aquarius, a symbol of purification from original sin through Baptism, that was considered the salvation of humanity, symbolized by Pisces.

"This interpretation explains the presence of the zodiac inside the Baptistry of San Giovanni and the Basilica of San Miniato al Monte," Bartolini concludes.

Astrology remained a popular subject among Christian elites throughout the Middle Ages. Renowned astrologer Guido Bonatti used his skills to advise government officials in Florence, Siena, and beyond during the thirteenth century. Florentine humanist and priest Marsilio Ficino wrote about astrological magic, medicine, and talismans in his *Three Books on Life* published in 1489, but made sure to remind his audience that it was God who made such workings effective. "In performing any work let us hope for and seek the fruit of the work principally from Him," Ficino writes, "who made both the celestials and those things which are contained in the heavens, who gave them their power, and who always moves and preserves them." Meanwhile, at the University of Bologna, professors were teaching physicians how astrology could inform their medical practice.

As scholars and theologians were debating and dedicating themselves to the discipline of astrology, the masses continued to engage with the heavens. "Usually the popular form [of astrology] referred more to phases of the moon than to motions of the other heavenly bodies, for the fairly simple reason that the moon could more easily be seen and its movements more readily understood," Richard Kieckhefer writes in *Magic in the Middle Ages*. "Detailed charts told which days of the lunar cycle were good or bad for various activities."

It was not until the early modern era that astrology and other forms of divination would come under increasing scrutiny of the Church. But that still didn't stop elites and everyday people alike from practicing their own forms of practical magic.

The Museo Internazionale dei Tarocchi is known as the "witch house" by its neighbors. Nestled in the bucolic province of Bologna, this museum dedicated to tarot lies behind the doors of an austere stone home perched on a hill. Upon arrival, I was ushered into the museum proper by founders Morena Poltronieri and Ernesto Fazioli, who have written multiple books on magic, tarot, and witchcraft and even created a tarot tourism guide of Italy.

Inside the small but beautifully curated museum, there are two floors of artistic interpretations of the major and minor arcana. More decks than I've ever seen in one place are stacked in glass cases. (A deck of cat tarot featuring ukiyo-e master Utagawa Kuniyoshi's work was the most memorable.) Downstairs, the oldest examples of tarot imagery are mounted on the wall, guarded by a figure in Renaissance garb.

Walking through the tarot museum, I was struck by the creative breadth of the practice. There are infinite ways artists have explored tarot archetypes—I saw paintings, sculptures, films, fashion, and food inspired by the tarot on display—as there are infinite ways to incorporate the reading of tarot as a discipline. These days, it can be as much a creative or therapeutic tool as a method of divination.

The tarot museum has been open since 2007, but it was only in recent years that locals dared enter, Fazioli told me with an incredulous laugh. (Hence its designation as the "witch house.") Many people still don't understand the art and science of tarot in Italy, Fazioli observed, and associate it only with fortune-telling. Apparently, Italians haven't yet given themselves over to the recent tarot renaissance to the extent those from the US and UK have.

The tarot we know today is a direct descendant of the Italian card game of *tarocchi*. Some of the oldest known Italian tarot decks, the Visconti-Sforza decks, were commissioned by the duke of Milan for various auspicious occasions in his family's life. An early set was populated with deities from Greek mythology, but later decks evolved to depict archetypes from Roman antiquity and medieval court life. A surviving Visconti deck from c. 1450–80 consists of four suits of fourteen cards (minor arcana cards) and twenty-two trump cards (major arcana cards), which squares with the seventy-eight-card tarot decks that are in use today.

The tarot continued to change centuries after its inception, sometimes for political reasons. Fazioli impressed upon me that the Inquisition's growing disdain for divination—particularly in nearby Bologna, which birthed its own tarot deck—led to the temporary removal of certain cards: those with powerful women like the Empress and the High Priestess, along with the Emperor and the Pope cards. They were the likeliest to ruffle the feathers of those in power.

In the fifteenth century, San Bernardino of Siena—a highly influential itinerant priest—supposedly set his sights on tarot as one of many sinful vices. His public speeches were literally filled with fire and brimstone, and it was he who originated the "bonfires of vanities," which predate Savonarola's events of the same name.

"With a large portion of local citizenry and leadership in attendance, these 'bonfires' involved the burning, in major civic arenas, of not only cosmetics, wigs, and clothes, as well as playing cards . . . magical books, amulets, and other instruments of magic, sorcery, and superstition," Franco Mormando details in *The Preacher's Demons: Bernardino of Siena and the Social Underworld of Early Renaissance Italy*.

One biography of Bernardino suggests that he had a special fire set to burn tarot decks. But that was the most innocuous of what he really wanted to burn. San Bernardino was fanatical about fighting heresy at all costs and publicly calling out sinners—especially witches—at his frenzied events.

"Through the staging of these spectacles . . . and through his preaching in general, what Bernardino succeeded in doing was not only to send to the stake for the crime of diabolical witchcraft women who may very well have been guilty of simple sorcery," Mormando continues, but "more important, he also succeeded in provoking or intensifying the general climate of fear and suspicion about witches that hung over the cities and towns of Italy and beyond."

Accusations of witchcraft were often voiced in the same breath as accusations of divination. There is a documented overlap in Italy between those involved in the practice of love magic and those who proffered horoscopes or divinatory readings. They were almost always women—and in cities like Venice, Rome, Modena, and Siena, they were often sex workers, too.

Divination became increasingly suspect throughout the sixteenth century, but under Pope Paul IV, books on astrology were banned, and astrologers caught practicing were banished from the Papal States. In 1585, Sixtus V declared all manner of magical practices—including divination—the jurisdiction of the Inquisition. His papal bull singled out female diviners and women possessed by demons, but did not directly mention witches. "There was no mention of *maleficium*, sex with the devil, or the flight of witches to the Sabbath," Rainer Decker notes in *Witchcraft and the Papacy*. "Only the pact with the devil was named, but again only in connection with divination."

The relationship between divination and Christianity would go through many periods of storm and stress from the Middle Ages to the Renaissance and into modernity. Like the wheel of the zodiac, popular opinion about astrology and the tarot is seasonal and cyclical. The sacred becomes the profane becomes the sacred once more. And, like the wheel of the zodiac, it seems we always end up where we started, looking to the stars and the cards to divine inspiration and answers.

SAINTS AND SORCERESSES

Siena, Italy

A SLIGHT SMILE PLAYS UPON HER SUNKEN FACE. Captured mid-rot, her severed head is preserved behind glass, eyes forever closed in the serene stasis of death. I watched crowds gather around a reliquary in the Basilica of San Domenico to see Catherine of Siena's remains. Nearby, her solitary thumb is mounted in its own separate shrine, another remnant of one of Catholicism's most fascinating female saints. No photos are allowed, so I entered the gift shop brimming with tourists to buy a signature prayer card that pictures her lifeless head. "O Catherine, most powerful Saint, neither the heart of sinners, nor Heaven itself were able to resist your burning faith, your words and your insistent prayers," it reads.

Although this book is about witches, it is, in a way, also about saints. They are two sides of the same coin: women perceived to have preternatural gifts who rose above their stations to gain repute, both ill and honorable.

"Saints and witches are made, not born," asserts Anne Jacobson Schutte. In *Time, Space, and Women's Lives in Early Modern Europe*, the author positions these two socially constructed figures as both strangers and stepsisters who had a certain kind of power, especially in Italy. "In the lives of early modern Italian saints and witches we can recognize some female agency," Schutte argues. "The lives of both were conditioned by pervasive male distrust of female nature as something 'other,' inferior, and potentially dangerous unless tightly controlled."

Catherine of Siena and, later, Joan of Arc (whom we'll meet soon) were both thought to be witches or servants of the Devil by their detractors. And Catherine and Joan would also go on to influence popular and clerical conceptions of witches—and which women were good and which were wicked.

Catherine Benincasa was born in Siena in 1347. At a very young age, Catherine showed signs of wanting to devote her life to Christ, restricting her diet to only the simplest of foods, and praying to the Virgin Mary that she would one day marry her only begotten son. Catherine railed against her family's desire to marry her off, and she eventually stopped eating altogether, engaging in what some scholars call "holy anorexia." As Caroline Walker Bynum explains in *Holy Feast and Holy Fast: The Religious Significance of Food to Medieval Women*: "In the medieval period, the control, renunciation, and torture of the body were understood not so much as a rejection of the physical, but as a way of achieving the divine."

Catherine eventually won her parents over with such acts of extreme devotion, and she was allowed to begin studying with a Dominican order by day while living with her family by night. At twenty-one, she would undergo a mystical marriage to Jesus. Catherine revealed in a letter that Jesus appeared to her and offered a piece of his foreskin as an engagement ring. Later, at twenty-eight, Catherine exhibited the signs of the stigmata, but said she asked God to make them invisible so she would not draw attention that might detract from her duties.

Throughout her short life (she died at thirty-three), Catherine involved herself in clerical reform and papal politics, eventually becoming pen pals with Pope Gregory XI and traveling throughout Italy sharing her message of repentance and rhapsody through God's love. Catherine was a pious and polarizing figure. According to Sigrid Undset's biography of the now saint and doctor of the Church: "Her supporters considered her a holy virgin, a visionary to whom God had granted special revelations. Her enemies called her a hypocrite, a shameless female, or a witch."

Catherine's old praying ground at San Domenico is but one pertinent place I visited in Siena. A ten-minute walk from the basilica through winding cobblestone streets is the Piazza del Campo, a shell-shaped arena in the heart of Siena, where the city's famous Palio horse races are held. This slightly sloped piazza is also where executions were once carried out, and where San Bernardino of Siena enflamed passions—and sinful ephemera—during his inimitable sermons.

When addressing his followers here in 1427, Bernardino fervently hoped he would soon uncover the witches he knew to be lurking in the city. "To the fire! To the fire! To the fire!" Bernardino declared. "Do you want to know what happened in Rome when I preached there? If I could only make the same thing happen here in Siena! Oh, let's send up to the Lord God some of that same incense right here in Siena!"

As Franco Mormando elaborates: "The 'incense' that Bernardino is encouraging his Sienese audience to raise to the heavenly courts is not the fragrant resin usually found in church censers, but rather the earthly remains of a condemned witch burned at the stake." Bernardino would eventually have his way, as many women across Italy burned because of his words. (Dina Corsi suggests in *Diaboliche maledette e disperate* that perhaps Giovanna the love witch was punished so harshly because of Bernardino's recent visit to Florence.)

From the piazza, I wove through crowds milling in the medieval streets until I reached the Siena Duomo. The Gothic and Romanesque structure was a perfect palate cleanser after harkening back to Bernardino's incendiary words. Although there are so many dazzling cathedrals in Italy that adjectives of admiration begin to ring hollow, the Siena Duomo complex is one of the finest. Words can barely decipher my emotional response to the towering, black-and-white–striped beauty (I call it the Basilica of Beetlejuice). It is without a doubt the most exquisite cathedral I have ever set foot in, and each visit is a pilgrimage.

Dating back to the thirteenth century, the Siena Duomo supposedly lies on an ancient temple ground once dedicated to the Roman goddess of wisdom and warfare, Minerva. Like San Miniato al Monte, the cathedral has a floor featuring incredible symbology—including imagery from the tarot. Set into red marble is a Wheel of Fortune tableau of men desperate to keep up with fate's forward motion. (The Wheel of Fortune is the tenth trump card in the major arcana.) There are also depictions of ten sibyls—diviners of ancient Greece—including the Delphic Sibyl, the Persian Sibyl, the Erythraean Sibyl, the Phrygian Sibyl, and the Libyan Sibyl.

Another gem within the cathedral is the cramped but colorful Piccolomini Library. I spotted an array of Pagan and Christian figures within its flamboyant frescoes from the early 1500s, including Diana, Roman goddess of the hunt, the moon, and childbirth, and Saint Catherine of Siena. In the center of the room is a statue of the Three Graces, Greek goddesses of charm, beauty, fertility, and creativity. Gazing down, I found the original mosaic tile design to be quite witchy: golden crescent moons set into brilliant blue triangles. Links between the Christian and pre-Christian world are around every corner, as are directives to exalt what is above just as much as what is below. The sky and the earth are given equal artistic weight and importance in the Siena Duomo, which is perhaps the most Pagan thing about the place.

Siena may be known as the birthplace of Saint Catherine, but plenty of other women captured attentions here long ago. Matteo Duni attests to the gender divide in Sienese witch persecutions in "Witchcraft and Witch Hunting in Late Medieval and Early Modern Italy," noting that "women represented an astonishing 99% of those accused of *maleficium* (harmful magic), as well as the overwhelming majority of healers." This legacy of female power and persecution still survives in Siena's structures and in its stories. A stunning city where divine goddesses, wicked witches, and holy female saints mingle, Siena reminds us that the boundaries between good and evil—particularly when it comes to women—are often arbitrary and illusory.

MIDSUMMER IN LIGURIA
Triora and Genoa, Italy

THE STONES WERE SINGING. The sound of my leather heels on rock reverberating through the narrow streets and water drip, drip, dripping from the ancient well joined the earthly cacophony. I haunted the outer rim of Triora, and there was nothing but the rhythm of my steps to accompany me. Wood was warping, roofs had caved in, walls had rotted away, but the stones remained. Slick with cast-off water, bruised by the scuffling of thousands over a thousand years, they had much to say.

I peered into the center of an abandoned home overgrown with weeds, flowers, and trees. It was here near the town border the stones began to speak. Moved to lie on the ground and take in the alpine scene, I let their voices overtake me in waves. They had been the bedrock, and they had been the buildings. In their simplest form, they protected the poorest from the elements, but they couldn't protect them from the people. I pressed my palms onto their smooth facade so I might feel what they felt; roughness sanded down by time, like the sharpness of the horrors that transpired here.

On the day before the summer solstice, I took a treacherous drive up to Triora. Tucked away in a plum location near the French border high in the Italian Alps, Triora is a picturesque village in a region once home to the Ligurians, the Celts, the Celto-Ligurians, and, later, the Romans. Now, it is known as the land of bread and witches.

My visit coincided with a festival celebrating Litha and the summer solstice, and the town was transformed into a neo-Pagan paradise. Tables were set up selling witchy wares, like wooden spirit boards, Baphomet statues, crystals, and hand-painted cat portraits. A tent with a sign that read *"Sensitiva"* offered readings. Magical workshops from the "History and Myth of the Mandragora" to classes on tarot, pendulum magic, numerology, and local herbs were held throughout the day.

A century before Salem, Triora became the breeding ground for paranoia, intercommunity strife, and fear of diabolical witchcraft. Although the borough was prospering in the sixteenth century, by 1587, tensions were rising. Famine set in. Some historians suggest it was landowners raising the cost of crops to fill their coffers who were to blame. But regardless of what spurred the food shortage, people were going hungry. Looking for the cause of their misfortune, Triora did what much of Europe did during the witch hunts: blamed the most marginalized among them. Triora set its sights on a group of impoverished women who lived on the outskirts of town in the Cabotina district: they were mostly peasants, single mothers, and sex workers.

To begin an official investigation into witchcraft, the town pooled resources to pay for an inquisitor from Genoa. Soon after, parishioners in a fear-induced frenzy pointed out well over a dozen women they believed to be guilty during mass one day. Subsequent confessions extracted through torture confirmed local suspicions that witches were casting spells and killing children.

The accusations began to bleed into the upper echelons of society. Some thirty people ended up in jail. It was no longer just the poor and the outcast from the Cabotina, but the wives, mothers, and sisters of landowners who were caught in the cross fire—and a few men, too. Giulio Scribani, an overzealous commissioner that Genovese officials assigned to oversee the case, began to ratchet up the torture. Some of the accused women were transferred to prison in Genoa, only to recant their admissions of guilt. Amid growing hysteria, village authorities began to back down when they realized what was happening, but not before a few women had already died from torture or suicide. Most of the accused were not executed, but at least four burned at the stake.

For a long time, what happened in this small town in the Ligurian mountains was a stain on its reputation. That is, until a few folks in the late twentieth century decided to flip the script—just as they had in Salem. These days, Triora is a haven for practicing witches, witch conferences, and neo-Pagan festivals. The town hosts seasonal celebrations for Lammas, Litha, Beltane, Samhain, and Mabon, as well as Strigora—a portmanteau of Triora and *streghe*—which honors witches every year in mid-August.

Triora still honors its witch-hunting past, too. The San Bernardino Church depicts witches in one of its frescoes, and two museums delve into the sixteenth-century witch hunt: Museo di Triora Etnografico e Della Stregoneria and Museo Etnostorico Della Stregoneria, the latter housed in the restored Palazzo Stella, where the witch trials took place.

Weaving through the festival, I stopped into an emporium selling local delicacies near the edge of town. There was homemade bread and pesto and limoncello—the usual suspects—and there were witchy sweets. I weighed my options: "Kiss of the Witch" or "Balls of the Devil," two different chocolate hazelnut bonbons. The woman behind the counter enunciated their names in English, beaming and gesturing to the treats laid out on the table. I couldn't decide, so let both melt in my mouth as I went in search of the Cabotina, passing shops selling witch hats, witch shirts, and witch statuettes on the way. As in Salem, the commercial side of Triora is off-putting—some of the same mass-produced merchandise is actually for sale in both places—but it's a bit less bothersome amid such incredible views.

On painted doorways black cats arched and witches posed, leading me through the town's medieval curvature. I stopped to take in the dazzling scenery of the mountains on all sides once I finally reached the Cabotina. What's left of the poorest part of town is a crumbling structure of stone and wood. The vegetation is thick, and fuchsia wildflowers spring up all around. Birds flitted from one tree to the next as I sat in the dewy grass, sun hat tipped down low to shield me from the sheer force of the midsummer sun. It was hard to imagine that evil was thought to emanate from this very place.

The festivities were about to begin, so I followed the sounds from the town square back to the heart of Triora. The band Bards from Yesterday was warming up the crowd as some sat eating prosciutto on slices of bread and quaffing beer. I was surprised to hear Irish folk songs from "Whiskey in the Jar" to "Drunken Sailor" at a festival in Italy, but given the Celtic history of the region and the impact of English and Irish culture on contemporary witchcraft, I suppose it really wasn't so out of place.

A few hours later, a torchlit procession of revelers snaked through Triora, bringing a band playing medieval music across uneven stone streets and around homes built into the mountainside. They stopped at each of the cardinal directions, and onlookers gathered with their cameras out, trying to capture the fire dancer wearing a crown of horns set ablaze, and another spinning flaming hoops around her neck and torso. A woman in a red bodice and dress led the crowd in welcoming the light of the fire before a flaming wheel was pushed into the center of the town square toward a tower of kindling. Once its embers caught, a group began to encircle the growing bonfire in a dance, holding hands, as others played voyeur from the sidelines, eating gelato. The fire swelled and crackled; the crowd swayed in parallel motion.

The next day I was in Genoa, sprawled out on a leopard print bedspread, looking out over the Palazzo Ducale. It was the eve of the Feast of San Giovanni—also known as *la notte delle streghe* (the night of witches)—and a much larger bonfire awaited me. Down the street was the ancestral home of Christopher Columbus. Around the corner was the Piazza De Ferrari where they do not make sports cars. Gulls were gliding in off the port. Genoa was a mighty maritime power at one point, but the city now seems small and quaint with a subway line of only eight stops. I was staying in Torre Ducale, a medieval estate with sweeping views of Genoa. Two Medusa mosaics scowled from outside my door. The beams above my head arranged in a crosshatch had held the weight of the building for over 500 years.

Saint John's Eve has long been associated with gathering herbs and with gatherings of witches. Bernardino of Siena warned in his sermons of an unguent made from plants gathered during Saint John's festivities that made witches appear as cats. But there was a practical reason for rituals this time of year beyond the frightful lore. Jeffrey Burton Russell explains in *Witchcraft in the Middle Ages* that "June 23, which happened to be the eve of St. John the Baptist, was Midsummer Eve, the climax of the fire and fertility rites celebrating the triumph of the sun and renewed vegetation."

It was fitting that when I arrived in Genoa for the night of the witches an Albrecht Dürer exhibition was on view at the Palazzo Bianco. A German artist known for his witch renderings, Dürer is a master of gruesome detail. His *Witch Riding Backwards on a Goat* was a delight to see up close: the print from c. 1500 was smaller than I imagined—tiny even—but the wrinkled hag triumphantly astride her beastly companion felt larger than life.

Leaving the gallery, I made a wrong turn and got lost in the maze of the red-light district. Women hanging off doorframes and sitting on steps in skintight dresses kissed at me, laughing, as I tried to navigate the narrow streets back to Palazzo Ducale. It grew late, but the sky was still rosy, and children were given maps for the annual "Ghost Tour," which guides families in a walk around the city to learn about its historical witches, rapscallions, and ghosts. (The 2019 hunt featured the tale of two old rival witches who escaped western Liguria—probably Triora—to magically have it out in the Piazza dei Garibaldi.) A band began to play the entirety of Pink Floyd's *The Wall* with an accompanying light show in honor of the album's fortieth birthday. I watched and waited from my perch high above the action until it was time for the bonfire.

San Giovanni Battista is the patron saint of Genoa, so it was particularly meaningful to share this night with the city. Coinciding with the summer solstice, the Christian celebration neatly aligns with older rituals that once marked the longest day of the year. As Carol Field writes in *Celebrating Italy: Feasts, Festivals, and Foods*: "Christianity simply grafted the Pagan fires to the celebration of the Feast of San Giovanni. . . . Bearded and dressed in animal skins, subsisting on honey and locusts, San Giovanni also resembles an ancient god of the fields, or the mythical King of the Wood who married the Great Goddess in dark midwinter."

Though I have been privy to fires in backyards, on beaches, and even in city trash cans, this fire outdid them all. Young and old, tourists and locals crushed in tight around the pyre's enclosure. Safety officials kept a watchful eye on the large pieces of kindling that began to burn, but somehow their presence didn't get in the way of the shared wonder and excitement that rose with a crescendo as a giant blaze tore into the sky. Hundreds of us were showered in flaming pieces of ash and detritus that dive-bombed onto hair and clothing. We laughed, dusted the fire's excrement off, and pushed closer, nearer to the flames.

Some in the crowd stood transfixed by the fire, arms outstretched, worshipful. Others were desperate to document the action with phones high in the air. An accordion and fiddle duo playing folk music erupted as the burn intensified. I saw a woman costumed in a cloak and pointed witch hat entranced by the flames. Children were hoisted onto parents' shoulders, awestruck.

The previous night's bonfire in Triora was partly a performance, with a select few fully engaged in the neo-Pagan ritual as the rest of us watched. But in Genoa, there were no spectators. Everyone was intimately involved. For hours, a single pulsing element held our thrall. People linked arms skipping in circles and switching partners. Laughter and loud exclamations charged the night air. It was enchanting and ritualistic in the most natural of ways. It was the uninitiated magic of community creating synergy between strangers. It was the purest kind of ritual—as most participants weren't consciously there to *engage in ritual* at all. I watched the fire until it was embers, long after midnight, and left with my hair and clothes smelling of smoke, the strains of violin and accordion still echoing across the piazza.

My midsummer weekend came to a close the next morning in Porto Venere. A train and a ferry ride away from Genoa, it holds some of Liguria's most sacred gems: sublime pesto, supple focaccia, and a resplendent medieval church built into a sea cliff on land once consecrated to Venus. Here, Romantic aesthete Lord Byron—who wrote of witches himself—once spent time swimming in the waters, writing on the rocks, sunbathing on the shores.

I climbed too many steps in the scalding heat to enter the Church of Saint Peter. Taking in the humid silence, I left an offering and lit a candle for Venus, the namesake of the port, and saw the sea peeking between stone pillars, a dazzling cerulean over a thousand feet below. The church may be Christian in form and function, but it feels like a shrine to the salt and foam and fertile waters that birthed the Roman goddess of love. Alone in a pew in Saint Peter's, I breathed in the residue that lingered from a millennium of worship. My entire body was slick with sweat and the marble floor was slippery under my feet when I finally got up to leave. Steadying myself on the church's striped walls, I began to walk down a ragged staircase cut into the cliff. The heels of my boots coaxed the stones to sing once more as I returned to the sea to continue my journey.

A WITCH'S GUIDE TO THE VATICAN
Vatican City

"WITCH TOURISM" IN VATICAN CITY is . . . complicated. I can hear the discontents already. Why would any self-respecting witch traveler dare enter the dark heart of an organization that has inspired the suffering of untold people because of its pernicious whims and intractable dogma? As with much of witch-hunting history, there is more to the story than meets the eye. For those intrepid souls desiring to hack their way through the hoary jungles of heresy to come face-to-face with the institution that once stoked the fires of witch persecution, the Vatican is your ground zero.

Visiting the Vatican most any day of the year involves intimate contact of some kind. It is stuffy, it is crowded, and I found myself brushing up against many strangers in a nonconsensual orgy of Christian ardor. When it's particularly jammed, the masses making their pilgrimage through the seat of Catholicism become forcibly trapped in the corridors in between when certain rooms like the Sistine Chapel become overpacked. To prepare myself for the crush of visitors, I secreted in a snack for sustenance, carried my favorite apotropaic charm for protection, and draped myself in modest coverings to ensure I'd be allowed inside.

So opulent it's overwhelming, the Vatican boasts multiple galleries and museums, gardens, villas, chapels, and one monumental basilica. Faced with this remarkable array of choices, there is only one option: go heathen or go home.

Contrary to what some might think, pre-Christian deities are cheerfully present in much of the Vatican—as are Christian icons who figure prominently in neo-Paganism. Once inside, I began by asking my tour guide to point out a few of my favorite Christian "witches." My first stop was the Pinacoteca Gallery to see Eve towering above Adam in Eden. Fingering a snake with one hand, she offers her man a bite of juicy truth with the other in Wenzel Peter's painting *Adam and Eve in the Garden of Eden*.

Next, I sought out the stigmata-bearing Saint Catherine of Siena, portrayed in Francesco Messina's bronze sculpture *Santa Caterina da Siena* in the Collection of Contemporary Art. Near Catherine, the depiction of another immortal beloved saint was captivating fans. Odilon Redon's portrait of the teenage witch wonder, *Sainte Jeanne d'Arc*, is housed in the same collection.

Satisfied with Christians, I spent the next hour having my fill of Pagan goddesses as I sauntered from one exquisitely decorated room to the next. I paid my respects to Greek goddess of love Aphrodite who is featured in a fresco in the Room of the Aldobrandini Wedding. I communed with Egyptian lioness goddess of war Sekhmet, whose statue is in the Terrace of the Niche in the palatial Courtyard of the Pinecone. And I stumbled upon Greek goddess of wisdom Athena on a ceramic kylix that depicts the virgin warrior saving Jason in the Georgian Etruscan Museum.

Poring over the Vatican's magnificent artifacts, I couldn't help but compile a mental list of some of the pervasive myths about witch hunting and the Catholic Church. When it comes to witches, misinformation always abounds.

Myth 1: The Inquisition is responsible for the witch hunts.

It's tempting to attribute the witch hunts solely to the Catholic Church, but without the secular—and, later, Protestant—authorities, the prosecution of *maleficium* would probably have played out quite differently. In the twelfth century, rogue Christian groups like the Cathars and Waldensians—as well as Jews and Muslims—inspired the Catholic Church to crack down on heresy. This new offensive inspired sweeping collusion between the church and state, and by 1231, heresy began to be treated in ecclesiastical courts as treason was in secular courts: punishable by death. This influenced the creation of the Inquisition, a formidable institution that still evokes the screams of torture and the flames of zealous persecution to this day.

The Inquisition was simply an arm of the church with the authority to inquire into and indict heretics of all stripes—including witches. However, inquisitors didn't act alone, but continued to collaborate with secular authorities. Sometimes excommunication or a variety of lighter penances would be prescribed. But in many cases, the smoke screen of the old decree *"Ecclesia non sitit sanguinem"* (The Church does not thirst for blood) was used to shirk responsibility for condemning heretics to death.

As Rainer Decker explains in *Witchcraft and the Papacy*: "In formal terms, the inquisitors did not themselves impose the death penalty . . . [but] employed a formula by which they turned over the delinquent to the secular arm with a request for mild treatment. But these were only empty words, for the secular authorities knew very well what was really being demanded of them."

While ensconced in the Vatican, I spent hours craning my neck and taking upskirt photos of statues or of frescoes high above, but my tour guide kept reminding me to look down. Upon entering the Greek Cross Hall, I melted at the sight of a magnificent mosaic centering a bust of Athena encircled by golden stars and the phases of the moon (a perfect place to stage a surreptitious full moon ritual). Sometime later, I spotted another beautiful Roman mosaic from the third century AD where Medusa makes an appearance with her glorious snaky mane unfurled. Pagan magic is indeed pulsing through the floors of this place.

Myth 2: The Catholic Church killed the most witches.

Although the Inquisition may have set the standard for prosecuting perceived heresies from divination to necromancy to witchcraft, by the end of the early modern witch hunts, the secular courts and Protestant clergy arguably had just as much blood on their hands. In fact, recent research suggests that some of the most heinous witch hunts raged in areas where Catholics and Protestants were going head-to-head, competing for followers.

As Peter T. Leeson and Jacob W. Russ argue in their witch-hunting study published in *The Economic Journal*: "Europe's witch trials reflected non-price competition between the Catholic and Protestant churches for religious market share in confessionally contested parts of Christendom." The authors compare this ideological battle of the Reformation and Counter-Reformation to contemporary Republicans and Democrats in the United States, focusing campaign activity in key areas. "By leveraging popular belief in witchcraft, witch-prosecutors advertised their confessional brands' commitment and power to protect citizens from worldly manifestations of Satan's evil," they write, "to attract the loyalty of undecided Christians."

So where are the witches in the Vatican? (Besides those of us traveling incognito, of course.) Although there are many "witches" in this place, perhaps the most witchy piece of art isn't any of the above examples, but Michelangelo's frescoes in the Sistine Chapel.

As I entered the chapel, the museum attendants requested our silence. There is no photography allowed, so I sat on the floor to gaze up at the ceiling and walls to take in their brilliance. Painstakingly crafted between 1508 and 1512, the central fresco of the Sistine Chapel depicts *The Fall and Expulsion from Garden of Eden*, which brings to life an anthropomorphic snake woman extending her left hand to Eve. The half-animal, half-human serpentine tempter holds tight to a fig tree with a thick, pink fleshy tail as Adam eyes her. There were plenty of depictions of the serpent with a female face before this rendering, but Michelangelo also bestows the Devil's snake with breasts, buttocks, and long flowing hair.

Around the outside of the central fresco there are a bevy of Pagan babes to behold. Michelangelo painted five sibyls from the ancient world: the Persian Sibyl, the Erythraean Sibyl, the Cumaean Sibyl, and the most notorious soothsayer of Greece, the Delphic Sibyl, a seer from the Trojan Wars who received her visions from Apollo. Just as saints and witches share certain attributes, so do sibyls and witches. As Jules Michelet writes in *La Sorcière*:

> In virtue of regularly recurring periods of exaltation, she is a Sibyl; in virtue of love, a Magician. By the fineness of her intuitions, the cunning of her wiles—often fantastic, often beneficent—she is a Witch and casts spells . . .

Myth 3: The practices condemned as witchcraft were a distinct form of pre-Christian magic.

The sorcery prosecuted by the Inquisition was a mix of folk magic, ritual magic, and nontraditional Christian practices that originated in different eras and evolved over time. Much of the so-called witchcraft that was practiced in late medieval and early modern Italy, for example, took cues from Catholicism, but was "often at cross-purposes with official doctrine," notes Matteo Duni. "The vast majority of magical practices included elements borrowed from church rituals," he continues. "Indeed, some of the most common types of love magic were known as 'oriazoni,' or prayers, whose format and language they mimicked." Sometimes, Catholicism and witchcraft made strange—but symbiotic—bedfellows.

I turned to take in *The Last Judgement* on the altar wall opposite *The Fall* and came face-to-face with demons crawling their way up from a subterranean hellscape, trying to drag more men down with them. There are no witches here per se, but the damned are animalistic, featuring the ears and horns and claws of earthly beasts. These tropes would be utilized in descriptions of the Satanic witch throughout the Renaissance, when she was believed to shape-shift into cats, dogs, and all manner of animals—or be accompanied by a demonic animal familiar.

Upon leaving the Sistine Chapel, I was right near the glorious behemoth that is Saint Peter's Basilica. A cadre of Swiss Guards in their fantastical period uniforms marched by, and I might have been spirited back in time if it hadn't been for the selfie sticks blocking my line of sight. The basilica loomed ahead, and I went through its resplendent doors. Inside, I was drawn to the Baldacchino above the Papal Altar, supported by marble pedestals. My tour guide pointed out the carving of a woman's anguished face as she gives birth on top and, on the bottom, a grinning satyr's face. She affirmed that there was another tour option to go below and visit the necropolis with the papal sarcophagi and Pagan tombs from the first century AD, but I declined. I had to save something for my return.

Myth 4: The Catholic Church was dedicated to destroying witches at all costs.

Throughout the medieval and early modern era, there was no single Church perspective on witchcraft and its deserved punishment. "Instead, there were a multitude of theories and ways of dealing practically with the devil and with magic," writes Rainer Decker. Contrary to popular belief, Rome was at times the voice of reason in many witch persecutions, not always a bloodthirsty instigator. As Decker cautions, "One should not speak sweepingly of the witch hunts as a policy of 'the' Catholic Church," or be taken in by the "'black legend' once propagated by Protestant, Enlightened, and liberal historians." The church no doubt contributed immensely to the persecution of magic and witchcraft—and popular ideas of heresy—but its role in the witch hunts has also been distorted by calumny and half-truths.

Once I had my fill of Roman Catholic drama, I followed the hordes to exit through the Vatican gift shop. While slowly perusing the gold and silver crucifixes, holy statues, saints' medals, and pocket-size bottles of holy water, I thought of how many witch friends of mine would make good use of these ritual materials—just as much as my devout Catholic grandmother would. This syncretic sorcery is nothing new, as many accused witches of medieval and early modern Europe sourced their *materia magica* from the Catholic Church, too.

Caressing the beads of a rosary I just bought, it dawned on me that of all the sites I had visited in Italy, the Vatican just might be the witchiest of them all. The irony was so acute I laughed aloud. With pre-Christian deities and occult symbology around every corner and a Pagan crypt sheltered beneath its floors, the Vatican is indeed a worthy destination for witch travel. For as much as the Catholic Church tried to wipe out witches, they remain very much alive and well within its ranks, merely hiding in plain sight.

THE IRON MAIDEN

Rouen, France

SHE ENTERED THE CITY OF ORLÉANS in the dark, an armored angel keeping her seraphim close. On a white horse she was a streak of light against the sky, a ghostly marquee signaling death to the opposition. In her hand was a white standard emblazoned with angels and fleur-de-lis. In her ears were the shrieks of dying English soldiers, a cacophony of saintly voices guiding her to free France and offering the seeds of knowledge that she would not live to see it all come to fruition. She knew an arrow would soon pierce her shoulder in battle well before it sliced through the air and parted her flesh. Joan of Arc knew that powerful men would bend the knee before her prophecies.

Jean Luillier, a burgher of Orléans, testified that Joan "was received with as much joy and applause by all, men and women, the great and the lowly, as if she had been one of God's angels!" Angelic was Joan in the original sense, when angels waged war for the Almighty. She preferred to carry her battle standard, not a sword, as her sharpest weapon was her holy guidance. And even though Joan presaged the deaths of thousands of English troops, she never killed anyone with her own hand—or at least that is what she professed. After a week in battle at Orléans, Joan ended a siege that had persisted for seven months. To the French, Joan proved herself a bringer of miracles, fierce and true. To the English, whose army suffered one of its greatest losses of the Hundred Years' War, Joan proved herself to be a witch. They said only evil could accomplish such feats. They vowed to see her sorcery stopped.

"Hallelujah, I'm a witch, I'm a witch . . ."

A new pop single was floating on the summer airwaves when I reached Rouen. Feminist messaging and genderqueer aesthetics mingled in the song's music video. "Virginity is a social construct" flashed across the screen as the much-maligned Miley Cyrus writhed on the floor in a red latex catsuit before holding a sword high on horseback dressed as an armored Joan of Arc. As I entered the city where Joan took her last breath in 1431, her influence was as palpable as ever, pervading the unlikeliest of places.

Rouen still lives and breathes Joan—Jeanne—nearly 600 years after her cruel execution in the town square. An easy day trip from Paris, the capital of Normandy is filled with quaint cobblestone streets and half-timbered houses. Upon emerging from the Gare de Rouen-Rive-Droite train station on a brisk, sunny day, I found myself walking down Rue Jeanne d'Arc. I wandered past a bust of Guy de Maupassant lording over a pristinely manicured park with water flowing across a rock wall. Nearby, the Esplanade Marcel Duchamp fans out in front of the Musée des Beaux-Arts de Rouen where a large Calder sculpture balances by the museum entrance.

Churches seem to decorate every corner of the city. Rouen's towering Gothic abbey dedicated to Saint Ouen has weathered to black around its face, giving the impression of rotting bone against the whiter, more preserved limestone. It was in the cemetery here that Joan was first sent to be burned at the stake. Before the inquisitors could set her ablaze, she signed an abjuration under duress, promising that the voices she said she heard weren't real and that she would no longer bear arms or wear male clothing. She left the grounds of Saint Ouen alive, but wouldn't make it more than a week. As I walked past the imposing edifice, the sun ducked behind its spire, then rolled back into place: an uncanny light show that served as a pointed allegory of the church's power.

The Maid of Orléans remains a martyr icon to millions. Just as the witch is an ever-shifting archetype appropriated for many a cause célèbre, Joan of Arc stands for so much to so many. In feminist circles, she is embraced alternately as a symbol of female strength and ingenuity; an icon of neurodiversity and genderqueer identity; and, to some, evidence that women can be conduits for the divine.

The peasant girl we now know as Joan of Arc has been the subject of countless books, plays, and films over the centuries created and re-created by people of all persuasions. "She has been claimed as an icon by zealous combatants of every shade of opinion," writes Moya Long-staffe in a biography of the heroine, "clericals, anticlericals, nationalists, republicans, socialists, conspiracy theorists, feminists . . ." There is no single type of person who identifies with Joan, and there is no single Joan whom people identify with.

My first inroad to explore Joan's saga was the Historial Jeanne d'Arc. The museum is accessible only through guided tours, and each one is an immersive, multimedia journey through Joan of Arc history and lore played out in a restored medieval archbishop's palace. Video projections dance across the stone walls, bringing Joan's story to life through narration and reenactments drawn from trial records.

It is mostly through her trial for heresy in 1431 and the trial to pardon her postmortem in 1456 that we know as much as we do about the Maid. But not all these details can be trusted. As Daniel Hobbins warns in *The Trial of Joan of Arc*, "the political nature of the original trial should put us on our guard when we are dealing with evidence produced by its judges—and so should the political nature of the nullification trial, conducted in a highly charged atmosphere." (Really, the same can be said of all surviving witch trial records.)

Strange as it may seem, Joan was not called Jeanne d'Arc in her short lifetime. It was during the first day of her trial in February of 1431 that she revealed her father's last name—d'Arc—which others have used to refer to her since. "The appellation *Joan of Arc* or *Jeanne d'Arc*, with its spurious aristocratic particle, gives a curiously remote and lofty impression, whether in French or in English, quite misleading as to the personality of the nineteen-year-old Joan," Longstaffe explains. "She never called herself Joan of Arc, *Jeanne d'Arc*, but wished to be known simply as *La Pucelle* (the Maid), or *La Pucelle de Dieu* (God's Handmaid), thus reminding her troops all the time that she was convinced, and wished others to accept, that she came not of her own volition or ambition, not as the tool of any clique, but at the behest of the Almighty, the girl sent by God."

Born in 1412, Joan grew up in a loving, pious family of landowning farmers in the village of Domrémy (which has since been renamed Domrémy-la-Pucelle after her). She spent her time learning to sew and spin, and her mother taught her everything she knew about the Christian faith. As a child, Joan was well acquainted with the mysteries of the spirit world. Just outside the town grew a tree suffused with legend that she and other Domrémy children would visit and sing and dance around, throwing garlands upon its branches. The Fairy Tree, also known as the Ladies' Tree, was hundreds of years old and thought to have curative properties, as did the nearby spring. Joan's godmother told her that she had seen fairies there, although Joan would never reveal if she believed this tale or not. It was around age thirteen, however, when Joan's sustained contact with the ineffable began.

Joan was in her father's garden and could feel a shift, she recounted at her trial. Sight and sound as she knew them were forever altered. Fear welled inside Joan as light poured into her frame of vision on an already bright midsummer day. Her right side aglow, Joan was told by angelic voices to maintain her devotion, as it would one day lead her to save France. Many times a week, Saint Michael, Saint Catherine, and Saint Margaret began to appear or speak to Joan, delivering messages about her fate. It was then that Joan took a vow of chastity to prepare herself for a life of Godly service. Shortly thereafter, she stole away from home, donned simple soldier's garb, and after much maneuvering, followed her voices to come face-to-face with the Dauphin, the oldest son of then-deceased King Charles VI.

Inside the Historial, the projections are positioned as a sort of parallel—a low-grade facsimile, if you will—of the visions and voices that overtook Joan. We can never know what her experiences were beyond what she told inquisitors, but it is only fitting to try to understand Joan's life by walking into room after empty room only to see them suddenly transform through sound and visuals, setting the medieval palace ablaze in light. Shadows dance, voices bellow, faces suddenly appear only to disappear, leaving nothing in the room once more. There were moments I forgot I was sitting among a tour group, each one of us no doubt hoping there might somehow be a different ending to Joan's story.

When Joan finally found her way to the Dauphin and delivered her messages to him, there was a known saying that France had been destroyed by a woman and would be saved by a maid. Joan never divulged exactly what she told the prince, but we do know that it involved his coronation and the battles ahead. At the time, the French had been in a brutal, decades-long war with the English and the Burgundians over what is now French territory. Hope and resources were waning. Whatever made the future Charles VII listen to a young girl dressed in a tunic and laced hose, Joan had arrived at just the right moment in time.

After her seemingly impossible victory at Orléans, Joan saw to it that the Dauphin was crowned at Rheims. It was reported that the two had a close relationship, but it would not be close enough to save her from death. Joan subsequently floundered in a few failed military advances, including one into Paris, and she was eventually captured by the Burgundians. They sold their precious captive to the English, who had been burning for the chance to burn her ever since Orléans. Kept in a cell where she was chained to the floor and constantly under the threat of sexual assault by her "guards," Joan the accused heretic was forced to submit to an arduous trial where her piety, her refusal to wear women's clothing, her voices, and her faith were aggressively questioned. Like other witchcraft trials in the fourteenth and fifteenth century, "sorcery was principally a pretext for political 'show' trials, as in the case of Joan," Longstaffe notes.

At the end of the Historial's tour, the final few rooms are dedicated to all of the Joans who have lived since the original passed on. The Mythotèque attempts to offer a window into the heroine known around the world through art, literature, film, and folklore. There are movie posters for Carl Theodor Dreyer's moving silent film *The Passion of Joan of Arc*, alongside *Saint Joan* adapted from George Bernard Shaw's stage play, and *Das Mädchen Johanna*, a propagandistic German film about the Maid from 1935 that draws parallels between Adolph Hitler and Joan, untenable as that may sound. There is a fascinating selection of Joan of Arc commemoratives, like a vintage porcelain plate featuring her tied to the stake with hands crossed at her breast as smoke billows into the sky—a rather tasteless scene to eat from—and a stamp featuring

Joan cutting a gallant pose riding on her horse. (She was truly the first "witch" to be merchandized.) In addition to multiple paintings of Joan, characters inspired by the Maid are mentioned in the Mythotèque as well, like Brienne of Tarth from *Game of Thrones*, a prime example of the Joan d'Archetype.

There is arguably no female figure of the past thousand years who has sparked such inspiration, adoration, and commodification as Joan of Arc. We take for granted that she is a feminist icon today, but how was Joan situated in the gender discourse of her time?

According to some medieval scholars, Joan did not predate feminism at all but was singled out as a model of progressive womanhood while she was still alive by an early feminist writer, Christine de Pisan. "Because of the curtailing transformations women were experiencing and their reactions to them, it is plausible to see in the fourteenth century the antecedents of modern feminism," poses Alan P. Barr in an article for *Fifteenth Century Studies*. "Because of the extraordinary and outspoken role she played, it is still more plausible to find in Christine de Pisan the first of feminists."

In 1405, Christine de Pisan completed *Le Livre de la Cité des Dames* (*The Book of the City of Ladies*), writing about a fictional city populated only by women. The author places famous figures in the city from Mary Magdalene to Helen of Troy, Circe, and the Amazons to build a case in favor of women's strength and intelligence. (These illustrious women were split between Christian and Pagan.)

"In *The City of Ladies*, Christine exposes the falsity of the representation of women by the male authorities of the past whom she had been raised to reverence," Margaret L. King explains in *Women of the Renaissance*. Though Christine does not advocate for women to leave their husbands and take over the world, she certainly offers a radical perspective for her time by elevating the idea that women were as smart and capable as men.

When de Pisan heard what the young Joan was doing to liberate France, she was deeply inspired. Joan was an exemplary Christian woman, the writer believed, so she gathered together her feelings of admiration and composed the lyrical poem "Le Ditié de Jehanne d'Arc" in 1429.

"Joan's timely arrival, simultaneously to crown the Dauphin and to presage the liberation of France, provided a made-to-order elaboration of the major contention in *Le Livre de la Cité des Dames*: that women were at least the equal of men, historically stifled only by men's weightiness," Barr contends. De Pisan's poem speaks of light overtaking dark, seasons changing, and transformations. She couches the actions of young Joan in terms of great women of the biblical past—Esther, Judith, Deborah—before coaxing even the most skeptical of readers to submit to the greatness of the Maid and, by extension, all womankind.

> Oh! What honour for the female sex! It is perfectly obvious that God has special regard for it when all these wretched people who destroyed the whole Kingdom—now recovered and made safe by a woman, something 5000 men could not have done—and the traitors [have been] exterminated. Before the event they would scarcely have believed this possible.

But Joan's glory days would be short-lived. Within two years after the publication of de Pisan's poem, Joan would be dead. Although the accusation of witchcraft would not make the final cut, Joan was found guilty of all twelve articles of condemnation against her, which included her decidedly un-Christian connection to superstitions surrounding the Fairy Tree, her angelic voices and prophesies, her refusal to submit to the church's authority, and her constant company-keeping with male soldiers and wearing of men's clothing. This last accusation continues to be a subject of great interest and debate among twentieth- and twenty-first-century feminists—and is essential to exploring the enigma that is Joan of Arc.

Throughout her imprisonment, Joan was repeatedly asked to wear women's clothing, but she consistently refused. Cross-dressing was deemed heretical, although there were plenty of women who had gone to war in men's clothes before her. At times, Joan said she could not change her dress because it was God's will she wear men's attire. Other times, she alluded to the fact that she felt better protected against sexual assault in men's attire. We also know that Joan was offered a variety of chances to attend mass, something she deeply wished to do, if only she would change her garb. She refused even that. "I didn't take men's clothes on the advice of anyone in the world," Joan testified. "I didn't take these clothes or do anything except at the command of God and His angels."

In the past few decades, some have argued that Joan's gender variance translates to her being genderqueer or transgender. (The Maid is a significant part of groundbreaking queer author and activist Leslie Feinberg's book *Transgender Warriors: Making History from Joan of Arc to Dennis Rodman*.) As it is tricky to apply today's language and identity politics to a person from a vastly different culture and time, I have chosen to refer to Joan as "she," as there is evidence she wanted to be called a *maid*, a feminine designation.

Examining Joan's legacy means relying on biased documents whose veracity is not guaranteed, but it is nevertheless clear that Joan's gender expression was transgressive for her time. Many people with gender variant behavior or dress were assumed to be witches in the past, and many people who proudly bear their gender variance today self-identify as witches. Perhaps our contemporary understanding of the word *witch* is much closer to what Joan herself was, then, given that it is a term whose meaning is always in flux, ever fluid and shifting shape, used to describe a person living between allegiances and gender roles, between modes of seeing and worshipping, between worlds, just as Joan did.

In this contemporary sense, Joan of Arc is far more witch than saint. She had a playful, confrontational demeanor with authority, yet was deeply spiritual. She once jokingly alluded to her supposed ability of witchly flight when confronted by a skeptical priest. She was told by her holy voices not to jump from a tower and try to escape prison but did so anyways. Witches are those we allow to have flaws—and those we force even more flaws upon in many cases. Saints, on the other hand, are those who could never embody the purity on earth that we bestow them with posthumously. Witches are impossible to pin down; their attributes and aesthetics—good, evil, gorgeous, ghoulish—are ever-changing, conjured by whoever speaks of them. Saints are bound by the Catholic Church's beliefs of what is good and godly. They belong to the world of binaries, rules, and order. Saints are deified. Witches, like Joan, defy.

I left the Historial somewhat heartened that Joan was eventually pardoned and declared innocent in her 1456 Nullity Trial. But it was a pyrrhic victory—too little too late. With my back to the museum, I strolled down picturesque streets, passing a bookstore displaying vintage copies of Joan of Arc volumes in the window. A sweet shop showed her bowl-cut–framed face on a refrigerated case of macarons. Another restaurant featured a sign with her haloed likeness painted over its awning. As I neared the place where Joan was last seen alive, I came upon a store, Jeanne A Dit (Joan Said) selling shirts with her stylized visage on them, marked by a sign in English that read: "Jeanne is the courageous and combative woman inside us. Jeanne, it's you, her, me." The design was apparently inspired by a French feminist walkout against gender inequality in the workplace on November 7, 2016. The Joan on the shirt was modernized, but still unmistakably Joan. However, the attributes we imagine when we think of Joan—short hair, armor, white standard in hand—are not based on any surviving portraits, but elements pieced together from trial records. There is so much about her that has been lost to time.

The street I was on eventually emptied out into the Place du Vieux-Marché, the heart of Rouen. The cheerful square where tourists and locals were shopping and eating around a market selling fruits, vegetables, and roast chickens was also where Joan perished. I closed my eyes and saw a crowd collect around a scaffold. A procession of over a hundred men brandishing clubs and swords forced their way into Vieux-Marché leading a lone weeping figure. Far from the handsome scarlet and green fur-lined robe and surcoat she sported after Orléans, Joan walked into the square in a long dress with her head shorn, wearing a miter inscribed with "heretic, relapsed, apostate, idolatress" like a shameful crown. I watched her climb up to the stake, eyes riveted to the crucifix that a friar held aloft in the crowd so that she might die with the vision of Christ on his dying day, too. In front of her was a sign declaring all her misdeeds:

> Joan who calls herself the Maid, a liar, pernicious, deceiver of the people, sorceress, superstitious, blaspheming God, presumptuous, erring in the faith of Jesus Christ, boastful, idolatrous, cruel, dissolute, invoking devils, apostate, schismatic and heretic.

The stake was affixed to a towering platform that offered everyone in the square an entrée to her agony. The fear and hatred Joan invoked in the Burgundians and English were palpable in her treatment at the end. Even the executioner was unable to offer her the kindness of strangulation before the fire was lit, a small favor the condemned were usually accorded. Her cries of "Jesus Christ! Jesus Christ!" ricocheted around the square. As the smoke began to fill her lungs, she kept her eyes on the image of her lord and savior. His name escaped her throat over and over until she could speak no longer. Some English soldiers in the audience laughed. Many French townspeople cried. The executioner himself was filled with horror, as were many other spectators.

As Joan's body became a smoking statue, frozen in her final moments, the flames continued to burn. The fire's bloody fingers reached into the sky, sparking signs for those ready to receive them. Snowy doves bloomed from their blackness, white as the horse Joan rode, white as her armor in battle. They soared upward, flames transmogrified into holy symbols. The executioner felt his heart split open, wondering if this fire was a foreshadowing of his damnation for killing a saint. He rushed into the friary for answers. Others scoured their souls to understand what they had just seen. In her final moments, Joan succeeded in converting untold people who were forever changed from witnessing her death.

But in a blink the smoke had cleared, the square emptied out. I was standing near the last place Joan stood, marked by a small sign. Poking through dense green bushes, it reads: *"Le Bucher"* (The Pyre), "The location where Joan of Arc was burnt on May 30th 1431." Behind the sign is a modern, minimalist church, Église Sainte-Jeanne-d'Arc de Rouen, with a roof like an overturned ship—or an abstract upwelling of licking silver flames. Inside the building there are colored pamphlets in different languages denouncing those who once perverted the powers of the Catholic Church to condemn Joan. It was nice to see the church freely admitting the error in its ways—Joan was canonized as a saint in 1920—but, again, it was too little too late.

On my way back to the train station, I stopped to see the only remaining tower from Rouen Castle, where Joan was once held. Within its fortified walls, she was threatened with physical torture that was not carried out—although the damage had been done already through the psychological torture of her trial and captivity. I trudged through the gravel surrounding the tower, thinking of her bleak final days, heading toward Paris with a heavy heart.

My emotions were erratic in Rouen. I had never felt particularly drawn to Joan before, mostly because she distanced herself from sexuality so completely, condemning sensual pleasures and those who partook in them. However, to view Joan through a contemporary sex-positive feminist lens is quite limiting. When seen through the lens of medieval womanhood, Joan blossoms into a true radical.

But like so many people who defy gender proscriptions, Joan of Arc is far more complex than can be encapsulated or expressed by the word *woman*. As someone who also defies gender proscriptions and is equally ambivalent about having my own identity summed up by the word *woman*, I felt a deep kinship with the Maid upon leaving Rouen.

Most of the people—most of the women—executed for witchcraft over the past thousand years are barely a blip on the historical record. Today, they all but blur into a faceless mass invoked for a variety of political ends. Joan of Arc is different. She is the most famous "witch" figure to have ever lived—and the most famous female saint, too. In fact, Joan proves the proximity between witch and saint, as you can find her pictured or invoked as much in witchcraft as in Christian communities today.

At one point during my tour, the Historial Jeanne d'Arc's narration declared that no one owns Joan of Arc. That idea really resonated with me. Joan does not belong to Catholics nor feminists nor witches nor women nor French people, and yet so many have been drawn to her and her story. Joan would not likely have approved of any of us calling her a witch or a saint and idolizing her—let alone worshipping her—but remembering her? It is perhaps the smallest, sweetest gift we can offer the Maid who has given us so much.

NECROMANCE IN THE CITY OF LIGHTS

Paris, France

*And what shall we say of France? It is difficult to believe that
she is purged of witches. . . . No, no; there are witches by the thousand
everywhere, multiplying upon the earth even as worms in a garden.*

—Henri Boguet

WITCHES ARE ALIVE AND WELL IN PARIS. The pestilence they expose
is of the patriarchy; the blight they reveal is environmental disaster.
Witches overtook the Palais de Tokyo in the summer of 2019 with a
weekend of performance and visual art. An eco-feminist collective com-
prised of "good witches," Gang of Witches is "situated at the threshold
of the material and spiritual sphere, of the visible and invisible, of the
conscious and the unconscious mind, of humor and revolt, of resistance
and resilience . . . creating points of convergence, opening portals, [and]
questioning the structure of our patriarchal societies."

Gang of Witches raises issues of gender, sex, and culture united
under the aegis of the archetypal witch. Paris is now home to many
witches like these engaging with activist art and magical acts—as well

as feminists looking to witch persecution of the past for clues in fighting sexism of the present. But in the early modern era, there weren't many witches to be found. It was in French territories outside the realm like Navarre, Savoy, Franche-Comte, Alsace, and Lorraine where the witch was crafting havoc with her dark magic. In Paris, witches were few and far between. The city was instead the breeding ground for a figure perhaps even more sinister: the demonologist.

Christian demonologists have long been dedicated to studying the Devil and his minions. "Demonology was the 'science' of determining the power of the Devil within the limits imposed by the ordinary course of nature," Philip C. Almond explains in *The Devil: A New Biography*. Ever since Saint Augustine defined magic as driven by a demonic pact, the Christian discourse on the dark arts flourished. By 1270, theologian Thomas Aquinas—who cut his teeth at the University of Paris—had written what Almond calls "the first demonology of significance in Western theology." *De Malo (On Evil)* supposed, among other things, that demons had the ability to deceive the human mind and body and could take on corporeal characteristics, which would later impact hypotheses about witches.

Researching and refining their theories over centuries, demonologists did much to shape popular perspectives on witchcraft. But demonologists were not solely responsible for their ideas. Edward Bever asserts in "Popular Witch Beliefs and Magical Practices" that the relationship between learned demonology and the common folk was not a one-way street, and that "while demonology drew some elements from literary traditions stretching back to antiquity, most of the attributes it ascribed to witches came from popular magical traditions." It was a nuanced interplay of "high" and "low" culture and Christian and Pagan beliefs that would ultimately create the archetypal witch.

Nearly a decade after Aquinas wrote his foundational work of Christian demonology, the archbishop of Paris banned "books, rolls, or booklets containing necromancy or experiments of sorcery, invocations of demons, or conjurations hazardous for souls." Magic was already a threat, but witches hadn't yet gone mainstream. It would take a few more centuries for demonologists to fully flesh out the diabolical witch. And by the mid-1600s, sorcery trials were breaking out across France and its territories, and demonological debate was percolating in Paris.

Some of the leading figures in the field of demonology sprang from the Jesuit-founded College de Clermont, where young Jesuit philosophy professor Jean Maldonat taught up-and-coming thinkers like Martin del Rio and Pierre de Lancre. It was Maldonat's lectures in the 1560s that solidified a variety of ideas that became demonology's bread and butter.

Maldonat "confirmed the theological correctness of many elements of current witchcraft beliefs," writes Jonathan L. Pearl, "such as the reality of the transportation of witches to sabbaths, sometimes through the use of ointments, and that witches sometimes murdered infants to produce these ointments." But Maldonat was merely part of a much larger circle of theologians. "France's demonologists were not a random group of unknowns who happened to share a particular obsession," Pearl explains in *The Crime of Crimes: Demonology and Politics in France 1560–1620*. "They were, rather, a network of noted people who were committed supporters of the Catholic zealot party in the wars of religion."

Paris was the place where so many of these French demonologists of note were educated or employed, like Nicholas Remy, Henri Bouget, Pierre de Lancre, and Jean Bodin. In their published works—like much of the genre—the Devil is truly in the details.

Nicholas Remy was a jurist who took part in the witch trials of Lorraine and wrote *Daemonolatreiae libri tres* (*Demonolatry*) in 1595 based on his experiences there. The oft-cited Latin text "is a classic example of a growing tendency to treat witchcraft almost as a *grand guinol*, writing to amuse and titillate the reader rather than to argue a case," writes Robin Briggs in "Witchcraft and the Local Communities." Less than a decade later, French lawyer Henri Boguet completed *Discours des Sorciers* (*An Examen of Witches*) in 1602, which was quite the opposite of Remy's work. Boguet's book "gave extensive advice on legal procedure, and provided a special appendix to guide judges in dealing with witches," Briggs explains.

Pierre de Lancre, a jurist at Henry IV's court—and a former student at the College de Clermont—wrote about his tenure as royal commissioner overseeing witch trials in French Basque country in the 1612 treatise, *Tableau de L'inconstance Des Mauvais Anges Et Demons* (*On the Inconstancy of Witches*). "Few demonologists blended popular and learned witch beliefs as effectively as did de Lancre," writes Gerhild Scholz Williams in "Demonologies." "De Lancre constructed one of the most vivid descriptions of the witches' sabbath, including the image of children being presented with toads in velvet suits, to be guarded while their parents amused themselves with the unspeakable pleasure of the sabbath feast."

Another French jurist, Jean Bodin, was arguably the most read demonologist of the early modern era. His popular and widely translated book from 1580, *De la Demonomanie des Sorciers* (*On the Demon-mania of Witches*), is a thorough take on magic, witchcraft, and the prosecution of such practices. And yet, despite Bodin's popularity, the Parisian authorities "utterly rejected Bodin's judicial recommendations regarding witchcraft," William Monter writes in "Witchcraft Trials in France." This was also the case with de Lancre and his "evident failure to convince his parlementary colleagues about the reality of the sabbath."

When it came to witches, the French capital just wasn't having it. Paris birthed the age of reason, and Parisian attitudes toward witch hunting were quite reasonable. The French Inquisition was no more by the middle of the sixteenth century, and so the Parlement had the last word.

"The Parlement of Paris was proud to play the role of the prestigious court which embodied the spirit of the educated elite," writes Maryse Simon in *The Routledge History of Witchcraft*, "demonstrating rationality and a strict observance of the law and punishing procedural abuses committed by lesser courts."

Of the nearly 1,200 cases brought before the Parlement of Paris between 1565 and 1640, only 10 percent resulted in the death penalty. When it came to the crime of witchcraft, "the Parlement had an astonishing record of leniency," affirms Alfred Soman in an article for *The Sixteenth Century Journal*. This was true of torture, too, as "the Parlement used torture much more cautiously than did many lower provincial jurisdictions, where vicious abuses persisted throughout the seventeenth century and beyond."

But all this does not mean you can't find remnants of the early modern witch while gallivanting through the City of Lights. You just have to know where to look.

Upon arrival at Gare du Nord, I followed my inner goth child straight to the cemetery. Père Lachaise has been a favorite since I first entered its gates as a teenage fangirl in the late '90s, impatient to plant a kiss on Oscar Wilde's grave. But this time was different. For within the largest cemetery in Paris are also the remains of those who played relevant roles in the legacy of the witch.

An open-air museum of art and architecture founded in 1804, Père Lachaise is a sprawling expanse of mausoleums, sculptures, and memorials. Leaves whispered breezy incantations overhead as I slid through the gated entrance into the necropolis. Laid out in organized streets that separate the final abodes of over one million people, Père Lachaise is a city with a multifaceted personality. It is at once a joyful place of discovery, a tranquil garden, and a somber space of memory and ancestry. It inspires reverence in its visitors. Voices hum at a lower decibel. Feet are mindful where they step. Commerce survives in the offerings of flowers, pictures, signs, jewelry, or small pebbles exchanged for a moment of time with the dead.

I dove deep into the heart of the cemetery eyeing oak, maple, and ash trees, Gothic headstones, crumbling burial chambers, and pristinely kept mausoleums until I finally reached my destination. Between two neoclassical columns, a man in eternal sleep is watched over by an angelic woman standing above him in a flowing shift. Here lies the literary titan once considered *the* historian of France: Jules Michelet, a radical who introduced the term *Renaissance* into popular culture, writer of multiple volumes on French history, including one book on Joan of Arc, and author of *La Sorcière*, a highly influential yet factually questionable book that sympathizes with the plight of peasants and women accused of witchcraft.

First published in 1862, *La Sorcière* is a blood-soaked synesthesia of power dynamics and forbidden Pagan passions. Romantic and revisionist, Michelet's anticlerical work positions the medieval Catholic Church as the one true enemy of witches, who were Christian holdouts and devoted members of a Satanic cult. Michelet suggests the witch hunts were a means of oppressing women in particular, and that witches were actually wise herbalists, diviners, and sexually enlightened beings who hadn't been marred by Christian piety and prohibitions.

"For Michelet, witches were ordinary peasants radicalized by sexual violence and near-starvation at the hands of feudal lords and Catholic clerics," explains Marion Gibson of *La Sorcière* in *Witchcraft: The Basics*. "For the witch, sexuality is good and scientific logic must be followed freely. In this, Michelet's witches appear, hazily, as the freethinkers of the Middle Ages, heralds of Renaissance progress," Gibson writes. "They are scientists, especially in regards to nature."

Michelet's version of history may be distorted (for one example, he took the demonological suppositions of Pierre de Lancre and Henri Boguet quite literally), but his is a scintillating narrative indeed. It is one that would influence notable first-wave feminist writers like Matilda Joslyn Gage and Margaret Murray, whose own takes on the witch hunts are similarly revisionist and historically inaccurate, yet have nevertheless been politically and spiritually galvanizing in many ways.

As John Callow puts it, Michelet had a knack for "projecting thoughts onto long-dead characters, and weaving together scenes and actions that were extrapolations, rather than evidences, from the original sources." But we must not throw out Beelzebub with the bathwater. Ruben van Luijk urges readers in *Children of Lucifer: The Origins of Modern Religious Satanism* to "take care not to dispose of Michelet." Van Luijk credits the writer for building upon the ideas of Romantic Satanism that were percolating in the nineteenth century: "In an ingenious way, Michelet connects the folk medicine of the witch with the rise of the medical profession and the empiricism of modern science. Science has always been revolt, argues Michelet; magic, medicine, astrology, biology, 'all . . . have been Satan.'"

Shortly after publication, *La Sorcière* was, unsurprisingly, added to the Roman Index, a Catholic list of banned books. But those who dare to even dip a trembling toe into the waters of Michelet's swooning prose will be rewarded—especially if you view *La Sorcière* as a heady brew of historical fiction.

"Think of the power wielded by Satan's Chosen Bride!" Michelet declares. "She can heal, prophesy, predict, conjure up the spirits of the dead, can spell-bind you, turn you into a hare or a wolf, make you find a treasure, and the most fatal gift of all, cast a love charm over you there is no escaping!"

And that's not all. The witch was also a sexual libertine, flying free from the shackles of shame. She provided herbal solutions to poor girls who needed help with unwanted pregnancies but also to women who could not conceive. The witch was a subversive figure who proffered endless succor, never judgment.

"She is the confidante of deformities of body and of mind," Michelet rhapsodizes, "and of the lascivious ardours of a poisoned and heated blood, of morbid overmastering longings that fiercely torment the flesh with a thousand needle-pricks of concupiscence."

Michelet was the first to reclaim the *sex witch* from patriarchal clutches. He was an advocate for Satanic Feminism before such a thing could be named. Historical revisionism be damned—for Michelet's imagination alone I am grateful.

Before I left the long-dead author's peaceful, neoclassical plot, I laid down a little reading material I thought he might enjoy—and that would not exist without his influence—the French translation of my first book *Witches, Sluts, Feminists* (*Sorcières, Salopes, et Féministes*). Michelet's Romantic, Satanic, proto–sex positive feminist witchcraft of the past may not be real, but the vital art and activism it helped inspire in the present very much are.

I went on wandering through the lanes of Père Lachaise, stopping to pay tribute to actress Sarah Bernhardt, who played a witch named Zoraya and was burned alive by the Spanish Inquisition onstage; prolific author and renowned cat lady Colette, who once revealed that "elements of witchcraft, magic and sorcery" were a vital part of her Roman Catholic upbringing; and France's national chanteuse Edith Piaf, whose singing was sorcery unto itself. All these women were brazen in their creative endeavors, defying gender prescriptions in ways that rattled more than a few cages—quite in keeping with the witch archetype.

My stroll took me back to the gates and again past a stately bust of Honoré de Balzac, who himself wrote of a fictional witch figure in the 1837 short story "The Succubus" and used to walk the streets of this cemetery quite regularly. "I seldom go out, but when I feel myself flagging I go and cheer myself up in Père-Lachaise," he said. "While seeking out the dead, I see nothing but the living."

The draw of Père Lachaise lies not only in its ornamented tombs and tree-lined thoroughfares, but in the afterlife that many notables within its walls have sustained. Their influence fans out in golden rays, in imperceptible threads that tie so many of us together in magical and mundane ways. There is, ironically, the feeling of so much life in Père Lachaise.

As I prepared to leave, I inquired after the dead to guide me deeper into Parisian history. With the cemetery gates behind me, my ask was answered. I began to see the metropolis around me for what it was: a necropolis. For the past is everywhere in a city like Paris if you have a mind to see it. I hit the bustling streets and pressed onward, eyes wide open.

Walking through Paris is walking through history. Above you, baroque buildings that once housed renowned writers, artists, radicals, and occultists stretch skyward. At eye level, luxuriant landscapes fan out upon which these greats strode. Below you, the bones of the wicked, the wretched, the popular, and the poor lie piled in catacombs or laid out lovingly in burial plots. The past lives on all levels in Paris.

Walking through Paris has itself spawned an entire field of inquiry. While traversing the metropolis in the 1950s, French Marxist philosopher and filmmaker Guy Debord coined the concept of psychogeography: "the study of the precise laws and specific effects of the geographical environment, consciously organized or not, on the emotions and behavior of individuals." Since then, psychogeography has inspired a multitude of spin-offs—place-hacking, mythogeography, deep topography—all of which parse out the fraught romance between person and place. But there is an added layer to this interplay when magic enters the mix.

"An obsession with the occult is allied to an antiquarianism that views the present through the prism of the past," writes Merlin Coverley in *Psychogeography*. Such a view "increasingly contrasts a horizontal movement across the topography of the city with a vertical descent through its past." Simply put, a walk across town becomes a walk back in time. In lieu of a living witness, location becomes the medium to conjure altered states and alternate eras.

This approach has guided the research and writing of *Witch Hunt*, but was especially evident in Paris. While there, I chose to stay in the Marais, which helped center me within layer upon layer of French history. Over time, the area has morphed from the aristocratic district to the Jewish quarter to a gay enclave, never fully losing the residue of its past incarnations along the way. But aside from enjoying the old architecture, the queer bars, and the Jewish delis, I chose the Marais because it offers an inroad to Paris's witch burnings.

A short walk from my rented apartment down Rue du Temple, people were enrapt in conversation, eating and drinking wine on tables that spilled out into the street. A bit farther past the Rue de Rivoli and the scenery opened up to reveal a grand neo-Renaissance building. On my left was the seat of local government, the Hôtel-de-Ville; straight ahead was the Seine, gliding by like a lady of leisure; and all around me was the Place de l'Hôtel-de-Ville, a public square once known as the Place de Grève where executions took place. Today, people sit and converse, contemplate, or have a quick bite. In 1680, crowds amassed across the grounds now decorated with the scales of justice to see the most notorious Parisian diviner, La Voisin, transform from flesh to ash.

Back then Paris, like Florence, was teeming with skilled—and not-so-skilled—diviners. And, as in Florence, most divination was technically forbidden by the Catholic Church but still indulged in by the general populace.

"The former habit of consulting diviners, to have one's horoscope drawn, to seek secret means of making oneself loved, still survived among the people and even in the highest of the kingdom," wrote Voltaire of the reign of Louis XIV. It was during this time that a scandal of love magic, Satanic masses, and deadly poisons rocked the upper echelons of Parisian society.

The Affair of the Poisons is the name for a wide-ranging scandal that involved dozens of nobles and courtiers and a network of high-level diviners in Paris. Such women were masters of the magical arts and would be consulted (mostly) by other women who wanted their horoscopes read, who desired to prolong a love affair, or who wanted a husband dead. The Affair of the Poisons was rife with accusations of devious practices done in the name of sex, love, revenge, social power plays, and self-preservation. The web of intrigue reached all the way up to the mistress of the king, Madame de Montespan, who allegedly plotted to use love powders to keep his majesty's affections and, later, when that did not work, to poison the Sun King and another one of his mistresses. By the end of the tawdry affair, over three hundred people were arrested and questioned, and thirty-six had been sentenced to death.

One of the most powerful diviners involved was Catherine Montvoisin, called La Voisin. For her high-ranking clientele she was known to use wax images, menstrual blood, and the hearts of animals as the raw materials for love spells, but urine, she believed, was best suited for banishing spells—or, more specifically, getting rid of an abusive or unwanted husband. La Voisin had been providing horoscopes and reading palms since the age of nine and had made quite a good living as a diviner to the rich. In addition to catering to women's love lives, she proffered reproductive services, too, and admitted to assisting with thousands of abortions—the practice of which, at the time, was a capital crime. But poison was La Voisin's specialty, and she was able to slip it into everything, from clothing and paper to bouquets of flowers.

I took one last panoramic spin around the Place de l'Hôtel-de-Ville. The weather was serene and sunny, and there were no screaming onlookers gnashing their teeth to see women burned alive for directing their magic to destroy men. A busker singing Lady Gaga serenaded me as I sauntered across the Pont d'Arcole, where boats disappeared then reappeared beneath my feet. Up a ways was a looming Gothic fortress, the Conciergerie, where a few renowned diviners spent their last days, and where Marie Antoinette did, too. Straight ahead was the ailing Notre Dame, which remained closed after a devastating fire. In its sanctuary is a barrel still stuffed with Louis XIV's entrails.

"There can be no doubt that some of the activities practiced by divineresses in Paris could be defined as witchcraft," writes Anne Somerset in *The Affair of the Poisons: Murder, Infanticide, and Satanism at the Court of Louis XIV*, "and in theory remained a capital offence." But as we saw earlier, the Parlement of Paris wasn't so fond of prosecuting witchcraft and had not executed a witch since 1625. Still, the workings of La Voisin smacked of the sorcery that once ran rampant in other parts of France—even if she was not explicitly accused of such in the end.

"While not extinct, by 1679 belief in witchcraft was on the decline in sophisticated circles, but perceptions of the devil remained extremely vivid," Somerset continues. "Therefore, when it emerged that divineresses and other members of the Paris underworld were offering to conjure up evil spirits for clients or to forge pacts with the devil, it did not seem entirely fanciful to accept that communications of this sort might be possible."

Many other diviners and their customers would eventually admit to or be accused of unspeakable Satanic acts, but La Voisin's name kept coming up. Even after her public execution—she thrashed and fought till the bitter end—La Voisin was implicated in further misdeeds. And it was her daughter Marie Montvoisin who unleashed a torrent of alleged truths about her mother's horrifying acts.

Marie confessed that her mother, along with an elderly priest, Abbé Étienne Guibourg, who himself confessed to performing child sacrifice, participated in a sacrilegious ceremony with Madame de Montespan. According to Somerset, Marie revealed that she had witnessed something truly abject:

> She said she had been present when Guibourg had performed a black mass on Mme de Montespan and that, during this ceremony, her mother had instructed her to hand Guibourg a newly born baby. Guibourg had cut the child's throat and collected its blood in a chalice. At the appropriate point in the ceremony he elevated this vessel and the blood took the place of the sacramental wine. When the mass was over, Guibourg had torn out the butchered infant's entrails and given them to la Voisin so she could have them distilled. The blood had been poured into a phial and carried away by Mme de Montespan.

Rituals this abhorrent became nearly commonplace in the confessionals of the Chambre Ardente or "Burning Room"—the special tribunal Louis XIV created to investigate the Affair of the Poisons. But although the inquiry lasted three years and much corroborating evidence was brought against the king's mistress and mother of his children Madame de Montespan, he never allowed her to go down for her crimes—or rather, he never believed she committed them at all.

In keeping with the Satanic theme, I moved as close as I could to the bas-relief near the West entrance of Notre Dame, still cordoned off for renovations. There, hidden among so many carvings, are Adam and Eve on either side of an apple tree with a serpent in the middle, tempting the two. The upper half of the serpent features the head and breasts of a woman—who some say is the sly succubus Lilith—but her bottom half is a long, slithering tail.

Scholars continue to speculate if all that Satanic sex magic really happened in seventeenth-century Paris. Simple love spells were certainly enacted, but could the devilish deeds described by multiple men and women in custody merely be torture-driven admissions or calculated attempts to offer authorities what they wanted to hear? Whatever the case may be, the Affair of the Poisons would lead to further tightening of French laws around divination.

Two years after La Voisin was burned alive, an edict was passed condemning diviners and practitioners of "pretended magic," thus suggesting that witchcraft, magic, and divination were not real, but merely tricks used to dupe the superstitious and vulnerable. "If Joan of Arc is sometimes considered as one of the first witches burnt in 1431," poses Maryse Simon, "the official end of witch persecutions took place with the promulgation of an Ordinance in 1682 by Louis XIV."

La Voisin's Satanic rituals would live on in infamy—regardless of whether they were real or not—in part by becoming a likely influence of Jules Michelet's *La Sorcière*. In documented confessions, La Voisin and those in her circle were said to have attended black masses where a woman's body was used as an altar. Accordingly, a scene in Michelet's book positions a woman as an altar during a Satanic mass, which Ruben van Luijk agrees "must have been inspired by the practices of Voisin and consorts during the Affair of the Poisons."

With witches and demons cavorting in my mind, I pushed past the construction bandaging up Notre Dame to the beautiful complex of the

Sorbonne, where the noted school of demonologists, the College de Clermont, once held classes. (The same building is now occupied by the classrooms of the Lycée Louis-le-Grand.) My time on the Rive Gauche was brief, however, and I soon headed back across the Seine the way I came, reaching the Rue de Rivoli, which led me straight to the Louvre. I joined the rest of the tourists to partake in a few pieces of witchy art within its walls, like Salvator Rosa's *Saul and the Witch of Endor* and the statue of ancient love magician Venus (de Milo). Hours later, I went north, parallel to the Palais Royal gardens, before finally ending my day's journey at the Richelieu branch of the Bibliothèque Nationale.

This marvel of classical architecture lets the light pour in through circular windows high above like so many suns looking down on rows of research desks. The witch has history here, too: this building was where the first-ever exhibition dedicated to artistic representations of witchcraft, *Les Sorcières*, was held in 1973. The Bibliothèque Nationale also happens to house a host of important witchy historical materials, from the earliest Marseille tarot decks to original copies of Michelet's *La Sorcière* to the written records from Jeanne d'Arc's 1456 Nullity Trial.

It was dark enough outside when I left the library that the Eiffel Tower was beginning to sparkle. I faced away from its lofty glory and ambled along the Seine, where the dead I met in Père Lachaise greeted me again. The water was dark, glinting diamantine in the moonlight, transmuting time in its current.

As much as mountains, meadows, and blustery seascapes, cities can be channels for communication between past and present, the living and the dead. Across Paris, I felt this dialogue taking place at monuments and museums, cemeteries and libraries. Intersections of space and time, these sites are crossroads unto themselves.

In many magical practices, the crossroads are a gateway to an Otherworld—a nexus of the physical and metaphysical. Witches have been associated with the crossroads since the days of Hecate, ancient Greek goddess of witchcraft, the moon, and the crossroads. Sixteenth-century demonologist Jean Bodin affirms that "a crossroads . . . is normally where witches place their spell," in *De la Demonomanie des Sorciers*. And in *The Black Arts*, Richard Cavendish points to a widespread medieval belief in "the significance of the crossroads as suitable places for holding sabbaths and making pacts with the Devil." Given all this, what happens in a city, when a thousand crossroads are layered across acre upon acre of lit-up land? What if your body itself is a crossroads?

Paris is a powerful portal; walking here an otherworldly ritual. There's no telling what you'll exhume or intuit.

THE GERMAN WITCHSCAPE

Harz Mountains, Germany

The starlight fades, the wind has died,
The dismal moon creeps out of sight.
A thousand sparks blaze in the night
As the witches to the Brocken ride.

—GOETHE, *FAUST*

TO GERMAN WITCHES—*HEXEN*—THE HARZ IS HOME. This mountain range, steeped in Pagan lore, offers an array of natural witchy wonders: the Hexentanzplatz (Witches' Dance Floor); the Teufelsmauer (Devil's Wall); and the Brocken, the tallest peak and site of the most infamous of sabbaths, Walpurgisnacht. Although most accused witches were executed in other parts of the country, this isolated region with a long heathen history inspired an entire genre of witchcraft tales.

There are no direct trains from any major German cities to the Harz. I transferred three times from Hanover before I arrived in Wernigerode. It was nearly midnight and the streets were empty. I watched the last train pull out of the station, the last passenger disappear into their car, and found myself alone. Cutting across a small park, I prayed my cell signal would sustain as I navigated the streets. Around every corner shadows danced, mocking my credulous mind. Creeping through a medieval town in the dark as a solo female traveler, nearly everything can shape-shift into danger. I found myself fixated on the region's malefic superstitions to take my mind off my real fears. Better the threat of a mythical beast than the reality of an ill-intentioned man.

Upon finally reaching my half-timbered hotel plucked from a German fairy tale, I slept safely and soundly. The Travel Charme Gothisches Haus is inside a building that dates back centuries and, like other establishments in the area, has a few winks and nods to witches inside. I rose early to continue on to the heart of the Harz, stopping by the hotel's Hexenstube (Witches' Room) for breakfast.

Heading back to Wernigerode station in broad daylight, I felt foolish for having been so frightened the night before, but the dark has ways of conjuring more than you bargained for. Next to the train tracks I arrived on, I found those of the Brockenbahn, a narrow-gauge railway traversing the Harz all the way up to the Brocken. (The only way to reach the top of the mountain is by train, bike, or hike.) I bought a ticket to ride and waited. A vintage 1931 coal-burning steam locomotive rolled in with much fanfare, and my descent in time began. I climbed aboard and settled into a seat complete with a map of the train's stops carved into a small wooden table. The Brockenbahn pulsed smoke as it pulled away from the station, and with it, human civilization dissolved from view.

The leafy canopy above became a verdant tunnel as the foliage grew denser. Beech trees gathered in congregation. Ash sprouted up here and there. The ground was dense with ferns and alpine flowers. This forest was sacred to the Saxons who once worshipped in the open air, in elevated spaces, and who made the Harz a stronghold as they fought back against encroaching Christians in the eighth century.

During the ascent, flora and fauna began to transform outside my window as we went higher and higher. The rhythmic sound of the train on the tracks became a mesmeric hum, dragging me deeper into the woods and further into hellish fables. Half-asleep, half-awake, I locked into the collective breath of everything around me and listened to the land.

This mountain is alive. The bedrock its marrow, the craggy cliffs that undulate upward a spine, the trees connective tissue. Skin and hair a skein of pine needles, almost noxious in their fragrance. Animals—mice, deer, wildcats, and birds—are the Brocken's blood, teeming, scheming, stalking among its spindly bones. The train curved up the mountain's back across tracks staked to her flesh, sliding between rows of tall, tall conifers like a lone finger raking through a thick green mane. Black clouds billowed from the coach like smoke from the fires of Walpurgisnacht that belch forth on the Brocken to hail the great below. Straddling my seat, I waited impatiently for the train to reach the peak. A woman made the rounds selling small bottles of brightly colored schnapps that some travelers gulped eagerly. Twisted sisters straddling broomsticks on their way to the Brocken would be in similar anticipation, their elixir a flying ointment lubricating their loins. Hair whipping in the wind, we were all unsure what delights awaited us at the summit. The mountain groaned in pleasure with the coming of the witches.

Germanic tribes were first to lay lasting claim to the Harz. Their temples and altars were trees and rocks, their gods and goddesses of the earth and sky. When the Franks Christianized and allied themselves with the Roman Catholic Church—the beginnings of the Holy Roman Empire—the Saxons were one of the few peoples who managed to stave off conversion, at least for a little while. Over a thousand years ago, their links with this land began to set it apart as haunted, heathen, Other.

The train chugged on through a vast expanse of spruce forest, and I began to see hikers with staffs making their way to the top. Not all have it so easy to reach the peak of the Brocken. Some choose neither locomotive nor enchanted object, but their own feet for their pilgrimage, as Goethe's Faust insisted to Mephistopheles when the two journeyed here for the springtime bacchanal.

"A broomstick's what you really need—Or a randy goat would make an even better steed," the Devil's emissary says to his human companion as they walk through the woods. "I find it very pleasant just to stray/Along the winding valley, then/To climb the rocky cliffs again," Faust replies. "Why shouldn't our legs feel its bracing thrill?" he asks.

The two soon stumble upon what appears to be the Brocken Spectre—called will-o'-the-wisp in translation—an optical illusion common on the mountain, where a shadow is cast by the observer from behind, producing rainbow rings of light around an eerie orb. The spectre is friendly, though—at least in *Faust*—and he guides the two travelers with his light to the top, where the fiendish festivities of Walpurgisnacht are in full swing.

When my train stopped at the final station, the steam engine noisily exhaled. I was a thoroughly modern witch of leisure who had reached the Brocken's peak not by broomstick, but old-fashioned rail. I climbed out of the black and red painted coach and hit the ground, primed to begin my excursion. In the sky, the clouds were diaphanous ghosts. The summer sun shined to no avail. Though it is only some 3,700 feet above sea level, the Brocken has its own microclimate that makes it feel as if it is nearly twice that altitude. At the height of summer there was still a bone-deep chill—but I had the fantasies of Walpurgisnacht to keep me warm.

Witches and demons and beasts of all sorts would brave the spring cold for they knew there would be body heat aplenty on the Brocken. Invited by Satan himself, they tangled tongues, pressed parts, and split their flesh at the seams in macabre dances of vice. When Faust and Mephistopheles arrive, they find that the "whole mountainside is ringing/With the witches' furious singing." They see Medusa and Lilith among the hordes, witches young and old offering sexual services, and amateur actors putting on the Shakespeare parody, "A Walpurgis Night's Dream." Faust is forever changed after he partakes in an orgy of wine and lust and laughter with the denizens of the dark side.

The exact origins of Walpurgis Night remain shrouded in mystery. Some historians suggest the holiday results from a confluence of spring fertility rites, the cult of an ancient goddess named Walburg, and the works of a certain British Benedictine abbess of the eighth century. This Anglo-Saxon missionary was Walpurga, who converted many German heathens in Frankish territory and was canonized on May 1, the day on which her feast has consequently been held. Just as summer bonfires burn the night before Saint John's Feast, the spring flames of Walpurgis Night lap at the stars the evening before Saint Walpurga's.

"For centuries [the Brocken] was believed to be the site of the greatest annual witches' Sabbath in Germany (if not Europe)," Gerhild Scholz Williams explains in *Ways of Knowing in Early Modern Germany: Johannes Praetorius as a Witness to His Time*. It was then that "the beauty and vastness of this rugged landscape was thought to be teeming with Satan's subjects, witches and their demonic familiars who flew to their annual satanic reunion to cavort in a space that was," Williams affirms, "at once real and imaginary."

The Brocken remains a liminal space. The interplay between Christian and Pagan, past and present was all around me in this beautiful national park rich with unholy history. Offset by a cluster of rocks centered in a circle marked with the cardinal directions, the highest point on the mountain is an ideal setting for a ritual. I walked the perimeter, dodging other travelers before moving close enough to place both hands on the jagged granite that features a plaque with the words "Brocken 1142m." The clouds were a gauzy blanket and the sun ached to part them, but instead remained a fuzzy mass just out of view. I headed downhill to see two rock formations associated with the Brocken's haunted happenings: the Teufelskanzel (Devil's Pulpit) and Hexenaltar (Witches'

Altar). But like a magnet, I kept coming back up to the summit, past the triangular signs with witches on broomstick that mark the Harzer Hexensteig (Harz Witches' Trail)—the path Faust and Mephistopheles might have taken to the top.

For Christians, Walpurgis Night has been a time to scare away demons and their devotees by lighting pyres, playing pranks, making noise, and donning the colorful costumes of evil in a springtime Halloween of sorts. For heathens, Walpurgis Night has been an occasion to honor the changing seasons, plant seeds, foster fertile beginnings, and hew to ancient rites that were all but snuffed out long ago. (*Heathen* is the loose Germanic equivalent of Pagan.) As I flipped between the reality of day and the fantasy of Walpurgis Night, I vowed to return for the festivities of April 30, which draw thousands of revelers each year. The holiday isn't only celebrated atop the Brocken, though, and you can find events across the Harz and throughout Europe. Now Walpurgisnacht exists as much in fantastical tales as it does in real practices. It is a flirtatious and fecund affair that has inspired countless creators over the past millennium to spin Walpurgis Night legends into music, poetry, paintings, and plays.

"The Walpurgis Night's artistic appeal derives in part from the pronounced cultural, historical, and political implications that have come to be inextricably bound up with it," writes John Michael Cooper in *Mendelssohn, Goethe, and the Walpurgis Night*. The eve of April 30 "is far more than just an event," Cooper affirms. "It is, rather, a highly symbolic cultural phenomenon."

Walpurgisnacht symbolism was taken to radical new heights in the 1970s when German feminists began to look to Walpurgisnacht—and the witch—in their activism. "This image evoked women as both dangerous to men and historical victims of male violence," Myra Ferree explains in *Varieties of Feminism: German Gender Politics in Global Perspective*. Inspired by the American "Take Back the Night" rallies against sexual assault that were popular at the time, German feminists staged their own demonstrations on Walpurgisnacht beginning in 1977. "The choice of Walpurgis Night, the historical gathering of Goddess worshippers, invoked not only women's potential power but also the European history of gendered political repression by church and state," Ferree elaborates.

I thought of these women as I traversed the top of the Brocken, boots caked in dirt, tuned in to the mountain's frequency. Walpurgis Night has been constructed with layer upon layer of fearsome femininity: mother earth, heathen goddess, female saint, wayward witch. These are the bodies, both literal and figurative, that birthed this springtime festival. Their auras permeate this space year-round.

Most Walpurgisnacht lore, however, has been decidedly anti-woman. Tales of witches flying to their sabbath at a high elevation can be traced back to the most notoriously misogynistic witch hunting manual of all time: the *Malleus Maleficarum*. A poisonous tract for detecting the damned, the *Hammer of the Witches* did much to define the witch as we know her today: as a sex-crazed femme fatale; a penis-pilfering shapeshifter; and a man-corrupting, absolutely putrid and disgusting hag.

Written in 1486 by Dominican friar Heinrich Kramer, the *Malleus* was a culmination of the work Kramer had done as a witch-persecuting inquisitor. In the 1480s, he staked his claim in southwestern Germany by burning women at the stake, boasting hundreds of deaths in his little black book. He was said to have indulged in lengthy interrogations about female suspects' sexual histories during a trial at Innsbruck and was eventually perceived as so dogged in his methods that he was forced out of town. It was after this expulsion that Kramer went off to the cloister to lick his wounds and pen his maleficent magnum opus.

Heinrich Kramer's treatise on witch hunting may seem excessive to modern readers, but was grounded in the demonological thinking of his time—with the sexism quotient stoked high to the heavens. There continues to be scholarly debate about the impetus and impact of the *Malleus Maleficarum* and its misogyny, but there is no denying the book made waves.

In "Witches, Saints, and Heretics," Tamar Herzig explains how Kramer's "characterization of the diabolic female witch, which influenced the notions expressed in the writings of later demonologists and witch hunters, created a uniformity of discourse in the witchcraft debate of the sixteenth and seventeenth centuries." Kramer did a lot to streamline witch hunting for both Catholics and, later, Protestants, so we have him to "thank" for that. (His sexism apparently had its limits—at least according to Herzig—because though Kramer hated female witches, he respected virginal holy women who followed in the footsteps of Catherine of Siena.)

In a bid to gain legitimacy for the *Malleus Maleficarum*, Kramer printed the text of Innocent VIII's papal bull in its opening pages. This pronouncement from 1484 decreed that witchcraft was astir in Germany, and it gave inquisitors Kramer and Jacob Sprenger—who is often listed as a coauthor of the *Malleus* but likely had little to do with the writing of it—the power to seek and destroy witches wherever they might find them. Innocent VIII's bull declares:

> Many persons of both sexes, unmindful of their own salvation
> and straying from the Catholic Faith, have abandoned themselves
> to devils, incubi and succubi, and by their incantations, spells,
> conjurations, and other accursed charms and crafts, enormities
> and horrid offences . . . do not shrink from committing and
> perpetrating the foulest abominations and filthiest excesses to the
> deadly peril of their own souls . . .

The *Malleus Maleficarum* is written in the same florid key of condemnation, expounding in detail on devils, incubi, succubi, and witches—who are likeliest to be women because "witchcraft comes from carnal lust which is in women insatiable." These she-witches partook in orgiastic parties at their sabbath meetings, but had to arrive in style. The method of their unholy transportation? Well, according to Kramer, witches would sometimes make a paste from the flesh of unbaptized children. Then, they would apply the unguent to a seat or piece of wood and be "immediately carried into the air, whether by day or night, and visibly or (if they wish) invisibly." Other times, they'd catch a ride on a demonic animal.

Before the *Malleus*, magical flight was avidly discussed among demonologists. As church law set forth in the ninth century, some women were known to have flights of fancy, joining a heathen goddess and her animal hordes in a night ride. The *Canon episcopi* explains:

> It is also not to be omitted that some unconstrained women,
> perverted by Satan, seduced by illusions and phantasms of
> demons, believe and openly profess that, in the dead of night, they
> ride upon certain beasts with the Pagan goddess Diana, with a
> countless horde of women, and in the silence of the dead of the
> night to fly over vast tracts of country, and to obey her commands
> as their mistress, and to be summoned to her service on other
> nights.

The official opinion of the church at the time of the *Canon episcopi* was that women who confessed to night flight were either dreaming or deluded by the Devil, not actually leaving their beds to travel through the air. This belief changed in the ensuing years and was challenged by the *Malleus Maleficarum*, but it also shifted shape, as Kramer differentiated between the oneiric fantasies of Diana's harmless followers and the reality of the malevolent witch's Satanic flight. Such vivid imagery would sink into the vernacular through artistic renderings that followed Kramer's wildly popular work. (With the invention of the printing press, there were at least thirty editions printed and 30,000 copies in circulation by 1700.) And thus, the foundation was laid for witches flying to the Brocken by broomstick.

"The Malleus did not name the Brocken or any other specific elevated locale," explains John Michael Cooper, "but its insistence that witches and those possessed by devils had to fly to their destinations and its several case studies involving witches in elevated locations evidently combined with the lore concerning the witches' Sabbath atop mountains to fix this image firmly in the mind of the witch-obsessed populace."

One Osnabrück witch trial in 1589 supposedly had dozens of women accused of attending a sabbath on the Brocken with 8,000 other witches. Other trials across Germany made mention of the Brocken or their own local version of a desolate mountain sabbath in confessions, too.

By 1620, Michael Herr had crafted the first known artistic rendering of the Brocken sabbath in a lurid copperplate. In it, some witches gather on the ground, some fly on goats, some on cooking forks, and other demonic beings wing through the air. They carouse, beat on drums, scream, and seduce. Casks of wine are at the ready, and a few magical gourmands surround a cauldron of body parts that a cat watches over curiously.

Further circulating Brocken lore, Johannes Praetorius compiled a popular work about the Harz in 1668, *Blockes-Berges Verrichtung* (*Tales about the Blocksberg*)—Blocksberg being another name for the Brocken. This would be the book that Goethe would consult in writing *Faust* over a century later. By the late 1600s, Walpurgisnacht discourse had been percolating for some time, and Praetorius infused even more sensationalism into the retelling of its tales, citing witchcraft skeptics and believers alike. (The drawing for his lively tome features a witch performing anilingus on a goat, center stage.)

As Williams explains, the "structure and content of the *Blockes-Berges Verrichtung* are very much influenced by the relationship of topography and demonology." Praetorius demonstrated the magical connection between land and lore in evocative new ways, Williams writes, helping to solidify the landscape of the Brocken to the general German populace as a "witchscape."

My time on the highest peak in north Germany was waning. My lungs were saturated with crisp, cool air, and I was beginning to wish I had warmer clothes on. Satisfied with my expedition, I stopped briefly to see the metal portrait of Johann Wolfgang von Goethe affixed to a rock (he wrote about the Brocken nearly as many times as he climbed it) before going inside the Brockenhaus Museum, which offers a historical look at the role of the Brocken in Cold War espionage, in Goethe's writing, and in German witch folklore.

Like the witch, the Brocken herself is a shape-shifter, transforming from mountain to military base to site of myth and magic. The museum's exhibition was educational, in-depth, and probably quite fascinating to a German speaker, but I spent most of my time trying to use the photo booth that makes it look as if you are soaring above the Brocken peak on broomstick. I can't resist a good souvenir.

During their time at the sabbath, Faust and Mephistopheles come face-to-face with witchy merch, too. They encounter an old witch peddling ritual materials and trinkets, the latter of which I like to think were similar to what I found at the Brockenhaus. The gift shop was brimming with witch pins, witch books, witch stickers and postcards, and small, multicolored hags on wooden broomsticks to hang in your home.

Because the Brocken represents a celebration of nature and feminine power and was never the site of murder and torture during the witch hunts, I allowed myself to go full-on tacky tourist. I splurged on a tiny old hag figurine, with hot-pink straw hair and a star-print sash riding a broom (who now resides on my ancestral altar). Her toothy grin reflected my gratitude for the experience of traveling halfway around the world to this magical place. Despite such commercialism—and the bratwurst stands and service vehicles emblazoned with the outline of a witch mid-flight—the Brocken retains a wildness that somehow hasn't been muted by merchandising.

German hag in hand, I reluctantly boarded another steam train to Wernigerode. At each stop down the mountain, I felt the mystery begin to dissipate. Soot from the exhaust swirled in through the open windows and sparked coughing fits among the passengers. I was a tourist on a train once more. The fires of Walpurgisnacht were no longer burning, but birds sang in the trees as we returned to the city limits. The landscape of the Harz is always in a state of flux, shifting from landscape to witchscape and back before your very eyes.

On my last full day in the Harz, I called a car service from Wernigerode. Within minutes, a van painted with a witch riding the word "TAXI" on it pulled up outside my hotel. Of course. I could barely conceal a snicker before greeting the driver and moving on toward Quedlinburg.

A dazzling medieval town untouched by the Second World War, Quedlinburg is a place of whimsical winding streets and over a thousand fully preserved half-timbered homes. The town has a rather feminist bent to its history, as women wielded great political influence here for over 800 years. In 936, the widow of the Saxon king Heinrich I, named Matilde, founded a convent, and the abbess of that convent would continue to hold considerable power in Quedlinburg and surrounding regions until Napoleon invaded in 1802.

Walking through town, I didn't see a single piece of trash on the ground, and there were few traces of witch camp—except for a small sign with a sorceress that said "buy before you fly" outside a shop window. It was effortless to rewind my way back to the Middle Ages while gazing up at Quedlinburg Castle and Saint Servatius' church on a hill in the distance, surveying the bright orange roofs that light up the landscape.

I had thought parts of Wernigerode looked like a German fairy tale, but Quedlinburg in its entirety is storybook stunning. Most descriptions of Quedlinburg in travel literature include the phrase "fairy tale," and true to the Grimms' classic German fairy tales—not their softened American versions—this UNESCO World Heritage Site has a dark side.

During my walk, I noticed apotropaic symbols like hexagrams and crosses carved into the beams of the aged half-timbered buildings to ward off sickness and keep demons and witches at bay. Like many German towns, Quedlinburg had its own witch hunts. But they didn't have nearly the impact as the propaganda that later sprang from them would, for Quedlinburg is also the birthplace of one of the most misinformed assertions about the early modern witch hunts.

Between scholars, feminists, and practicing witches, there have been divergent views on how many people were accused of and executed for witchcraft in early modern times. American historian Anne Barstow estimates 200,000 people accused and 100,000 put to death, but she admits to the difficulty of coming up with such numbers. In *Witchcraze: A New History of the European Witch Hunts*, Barstow writes: "Working with the statistics of witchcraft is like working with quicksand."

Australian historian Lyndal Roper estimates half of Barstow's number in *Witch Craze: Terror and Fantasy in Baroque Germany*. "Over the course of the witch hunt, upwards of perhaps 50,000 people died," she writes. "We will never know the exact figure because in many places the records of their interrogations have simply been destroyed, with allusions made only to 'hundreds' of witches killed."

German historian Wolfgang Behringer concurs with Roper in *Witches and Witch-Hunts*: "For witchcraft and sorcery between 1400 and 1800, all in all, we estimate something like 50,000 legal death penalties," he writes, adding that there were likely twice as many people who were punished with "banishment, fines, or church penance."

But others—including feminist writers beginning with Matilda Joslyn Gage in the late nineteenth century and continuing with Margaret Murray and Mary Daly in the twentieth—have bandied about the absurdly large number of nine million. Wonder where that came from? Look no further than the quaint old town of Quedlinburg.

Ronald Hutton explains in *Witches, Druids, and King Arthur* that the eighteenth-century German historian Gottfried Christian Voigt supposed that over nine million witches were killed in Europe based on the witch hunt death toll in his hometown. Voigt "had arrived at this simply by discovering records of the burning of thirty witches at Quedlinburg itself between 1569 and 1583 and assuming that these were normative for every equivalent period of time as long as the laws against witchcraft were in operation," Hutton writes. From there, "he simply kept on multiplying the figure in relation to the presumed population of other Christian countries."

There is a method to the madness of this astronomical figure, even though it is completely off base. But now that historians have roundly disproved Voigt's number, focusing too much on the exact death toll can divert attention away from unpacking the lasting legacy of witch hunts in the West.

As I took in the thousand-year-old streets of Quedlinburg, I let myself wander without a map. Elderly people sat outside their brown and white abodes, sunning themselves. A small black cat in a park emerged from the bushes to meow sweetly at me when I passed. But try as I might to get lost in Quedlinburg, I've found that medieval European towns always seem to deposit you right back in the town square.

There, the city hall or Rathaus has sat in the same place since the early 1300s, its stone face now masked with a thick veil of vines and flowers. Restaurants and shops line all sides of the square, and it was surprisingly quiet despite people sitting outside, drinking beer, deep in conversation. Refreshed by a tranquil ramble through Quedlinburg's medieval paradise, I was ready to tackle another part of witch history and continue on to Thale, a ten-minute train ride from the charming past to the kitschy, witchy present.

Thale is an ergot trip of a town. A witch theme park, museums rife with torture devices and psychosexual drama, and the notorious Hexentanzplatz plateau make it one of the most fascinating and absurd places I visited on my witch hunt.

Fresh off the train, I was overpowered by commercial offerings in the small Thale station. Crystals, candles, witch-themed liquor, witch-themed pins and postcards, and neon shirts printed with witches flying on broomsticks were everywhere I turned. I tore myself away from the mesmerizing call of merch only to discover the Obscurum Thale right next to the station. The outside looks straight out of a Party City on Halloween, but upon closer inspection, it revealed itself to be much more enticing. A skeleton in a black shroud pointed up the Obscurum entrance stairs, and on the wall hung a print of John William Waterhouse's *The Magic Circle*. My interest was piqued.

Inside this oddities museum, an ahistorical bricolage of fact and fiction rubs elbows in every room. A panel about the *Malleus Maleficarum*, a Befragungsstuhl (spiked interrogation chair), herbs associated with witchcraft, and logs assembled in a witch-burning pyre were near displays featuring vampires, werewolves, and zombies. There were so many rooms chock-full of occult paraphernalia I could barely see everything. It was an apt harbinger of what was to come during my adventures in Thale.

A sunny walk through a wooded area across from the Obscurum led me to the Funpark where my doppelgänger—a smiling blonde witch statue in fuchsia hat and dress—welcomed me inside. I passed a smattering of children's rides before joining families in line for the gondola that would lift us up to the Hexentanzplatz. Hundreds of feet in the air alone in my own glass car I had a panoramic view of the dense wilderness that permeates the Harz Mountains. Once more, I sensed uncertain shapes appearing. Sinister rock formations poked up like witches' fingers summoning me from the forest below. Within minutes I was in the place where the Pagan party started before it crescendoed on the Brocken.

Nestled high above the Bode Gorge, the Hexentanzplatz is a rocky plateau with strong Saxon roots. (There are even remains of a Saxon granite wall over 1,500 years old near the site.) This clearing was supposedly where the Saxons once held rituals and sacrifices to their mountain gods and goddesses, and it thus retains a heathen tenor, drawing countless revelers every year to the Witches' Dance Floor for its own Walpurgis Night celebration.

"We know that all over Germany a grand annual excursion of witches is placed on the *first night in May* (Walpurgis), i.e., on the date of a sacrificial feast and the old May-gathering of the people," writes folklorist Jacob Grimm in his 1835 exploration of Germanic myths, *Deutsche Mythologie*. "The witches invariably resort to places where formerly justice was administered, or sacrifices were offered," he continues. "Almost all the witch-mountains were once hills of sacrifice, boundary-hills, or salt-hills."

Like the Brocken, the Hexentanzplatz is rich in witch lore. It is similarly located in the Upper Harz region, an area once described as "wilder, its rock scenery more grotesque" than the Lower Harz in an 1880 travel guide published in *London Society*. Long before the area's commercialization, long before a theme park was built, Thale had "the best, but also the dearest, inns in the Harz." The nineteenth-century English travel writer goes on to describe the Hexentanzplatz as "a perpendicular cliff . . . which affords a yet finer view of the whole mountain chain." These days, you can indulge in this view easily via gondola or through the old hiking trail that spirals up from the lush gorge below.

Once at the top, I was overwhelmed by German signs pointing in all directions to different attractions. The Hexentanzplatz is now part nature preserve, part witch theme park, with an open-air theater, a zoo, a multipart museum, and many witch-themed refreshment stands and gift shops to behold. My first instinct was to follow the crowds, which led me to a central area with statues of a naked Devil and witch that children were treating like jungle gyms.

One young girl straddled a hunched witch figure whose protruding backside was home to a large spider. She steadied her baby sibling in front of her as the two giggled. Another young boy studied an animal demon at the witch's side, while other children posed with the Devil manspreading (demonspreading?) on a large rock. The Dark Lord's genitals are carved in great bronze detail, rubbed to a bright sheen presumably by visitors pawing at them for good luck.

Nearby was the Hexenbufett (Witch Buffet), a restaurant where folks were gorging themselves on fast food, right near the edge of a rock overhang above a thousand-foot drop. Shutting out the noise, I focused on the mountainous terrain that was at once alluring and foreboding. (I heard no other language than the mother tongue in Thale, and no one even tried to speak English to me when I fumbled through my awkward German.) Moving away from the crush of screaming children and their parents, I entered the Walpurgisgrotte section of the Harzeum. It was eerily empty and offered an even stranger mix of material than the

Obscurum. In every dim, musty corner, witch stereotypes came to life through creepy mannequins set against elaborate tableaux.

A solitary sorceress posed in a room full of potions and bundles of dried herbs. A witch mom and devil dad watched their hellspawn lie on the living room floor playing with a pentagram board game covered in snails. A woman in lingerie beckoned from a house covered in hearts and beaming red light. A wrinkled hag with long gray hair grinned in front of a cottage while a black cat perched on her shoulder and a demon peeked out from the window behind her. All the most vilified forms of femininity associated with witches—childless women, monstrous mothers, old women, promiscuous women—were represented.

Amid more witch torture devices I saw contemporary witchcraft ephemera—tarot, runes, and spirit boards—surrounded by cobwebbed candelabras and skulls. I spied what appeared to be death masks on the wall, in addition to a small child wearing a turtle shell as a hat. Right before I left, I walked by a scene with a woman in a wedding dress fanning out her credit cards and holding the leash of a man on all fours, because *every woman* is a witch in the eyes of her husband, I guess?

Darkly humorous and extraordinarily weird—especially to my American eyes—the Walpurgisgrotte left me a bit wobbly as I transitioned from the dark German fun house of witchcraft lore to a beautiful sunny day on a mountaintop. The epitome of the mythical German forest lay below, spreading out as far as the eye could see. Around me, families with young children seemed not to give a second thought to the surplus of witches and devils lurking about—it was all in good fun. I embraced the quite literal contrast of dark and light atop the Hexentanzplatz, keeping this feeling of dissonance alive throughout the rest of my explorations back down to the base of the mountain and returning to Quedlinburg.

The early modern witch—particularly in Germany—was entrancing but equally if not more so repulsing. If she had beauty, it only concealed rotting hag flesh beneath. I felt this unsettling juxtaposition viscerally in the Harz when confronted with bald commercialism offset by breathtaking natural beauty and the real horrors of witch hunting history masked by the ghoulish glee of kitschy witch museums and attractions.

I was constantly shocked, mouth agape, with no one to share my surprise. Horrified one moment, awestruck the next, and overtaken by demonic cackles at the absurdity of it all. Thousands of people died horrific deaths in Germany—the most of any region in Europe—and yet I saw little reverence for this history in the north. Or, to look at it another way, perhaps what witch lore I did see was more a celebration of Pagan beliefs and misunderstood magical women rather than a funeral for them. What I found in the south, however, was a completely different story.

TERROR AND TRANSFORMATION IN BAVARIA
Bamberg, Germany

BAMBERG IS A BAROQUE FEAST for the eyes. Saint Martin's Church spreads out in an opulent orgy of pink and gold. Pink marble pyramids bookend a gilded Christogram in a ring of joyful cherubim above the altar. Pink marble columns unfurl into gold scrollwork. The fresco on the ceiling is an eye-catching trick of trompe l'oeil that transforms the space into a soaring, golden dome.

Across town, the New Residence high on a hill overflows with the excesses of ornamentation: tapestries, state apartments, antique furniture, and masterpieces of German art and craftsmanship. A sprawling rose garden greets you as you enter and exit, its pink, white, and red flowers manicured into color-coordinated rows. The view up here of "Little Venice," its tranquil waters flowing between half-timbered houses, is breathtaking. Bamberg is indeed a city of spectacular sights, centuries after it was famed for a breathtaking spectacle of a different sort.

Fear of the witch in early modern Germany was as visual as it was visceral. Infernal female flesh falling off brittle bones, the slack-mouthed hag was a Satanic scold who mounted goats backward, brewed babies, and cavorted with demons. She killed crops, cursed pregnancies, soured milk and the marital bed. Her hag loins were no longer in working order, but she still seethed with forbidden lust just as much as her opposite—the young, nubile sorceress whose flowing hair was a thicket of Venusian mysteries.

"These preoccupations about fertility, women's bodies and the fragility of infancy lay at the heart of the witch craze in Germany," writes Lyndal Roper in *Witch Craze*, "and it was in German art that the image of the witch found its fullest exploration."

Some of the earliest representations of the witch in German art are included as woodcuts in legal scholar Ulrich Molitor's witchcraft treatise *On Female Witches and Seers*, first printed in 1489. Three sly sorceresses plot over supper. Half-human, half-animal creatures fly on cooking forks. A witch and demon tangle tongues, and two witches bring bad weather with a flaming cauldron of potent potions.

"The witches of the German witch hunts were first and foremost weather magicians," Johannes Dillinger explains in "Germany—'The Mother of the Witches.'" Although witches were thought to wreak all kinds of havoc on the bodies of the citizenry and its livestock, it was the vicissitudes of the elements that caused much fear and concern. "Time and time again, the only point of the witches' sabbath seemed to have been to give the witches the opportunity to engage in weather magic collectively," Dillinger adds. "In very many cases, a thunderstorm or frost that threatened a region or a village with crop failure provoked a witch hunt."

Hans Baldung Grien, arguably *the* witch artist of the sixteenth century, also depicts elemental sorceresses of this sort in his 1523 oil painting *The Weather Witches*. Two pretty, nude women and a demonically cute, fat-faced child are surrounded by blackening storm clouds. One witch stands with her back to the viewer, looking over her shoulder coquettishly. The other is seated, barely concealing a goat beneath her crotch as she holds a glass jar aloft in an act of spellcasting. Of Baldung's many works featuring witches, this one is undoubtedly the most genteel. Usually, his canvases are alive with bare-skinned crones, legs spread and crafting foul unguents, bones and baby parts littered about; witches mid-flight; and women of all ages fondling themselves and one another or interfacing with a demon in some sort of debauched act.

"Baldung's abject witches confirmed everything that men aspired to by representing all that they struggled to reject," posits Linda C. Hults in *The Witch as Muse: Art, Gender, and Power in Early Modern Europe.* The witch's perverse sexuality and destructive feminine magic that Heinrich Kramer describes in the *Malleus Maleficarum* is expressed both literally, allegorically, and erotically in Baldung's art—and in the art of his mentor, Albrecht Dürer. In fact, Dürer's own godfather published two editions of the dastardly text in the 1490s.

The Four Witches, engraved by Dürer in 1497, epitomizes the burgeoning witchcraft discourse of his time. Four seminude young women face each other in a huddle, creating their own closed circle of intrigue to which men have no access. A demon peers out from a darkened corner as the women no doubt are engaged in some kind of conspiracy. Male viewers would certainly see allusions to Venus and the Three Graces in this piece, Hults notes, as well as a contemporary vision of diabolical spellcraft.

"A masterpiece of insinuation, Dürer's image is the perfect embodiment of the status of the concept of witchcraft in the late fifteenth century as it coalesced from ancient beliefs in clandestine, orgiastic nocturnal gatherings, cannibalistic infanticide, and night flying women who followed a goddess to 'Venusberg' for riotous revelry," Hults writes. "The *Malleus* forged these beliefs into an apocalyptic misogyny, envisioning an organized conspiracy of witches and the devil against the Christian order—a sure sign of the end."

For many, this was not hyperbole, because the end *was* near. And the citizenry of Bamberg had no idea just how near it was.

In late spring of 1626, the seasons betrayed Bamberg. Frost descended on the fields, killing rye and barley crops, and boats froze where they were docked. Bamberg resident Sister Anna Maria Junius wrote in her diary that, on May 25, "a loud cry went up in the city . . . [and] people were frightened to death" when they discovered what had happened overnight. Prince-Bishop Johann Georg Fuchs von Dornheim, she noted, was "furious."

Today, scientists attribute this climatic change to the Little Ice Age. Back then, it was a sure sign of Satan's power on earth. Within six months of the frost, Prince-Bishop Dornheim had established the Hexen-Kommission to seek out the witches responsible, placing in charge suffragan Bishop Friedrich Förner, a leader in the war against Protestantism during the Counter-Reformation. Dornheim also issued a law which forbade anyone from criticizing or interfering with the process, and thus the stage was set for the great witch hunt of Bamberg, where about a thousand people were viciously hunted, tortured, and executed in one of the bloodiest witch hunts in European history.

Germany in the early modern era—much like France—was not unified within the territory it covers today. Witch hunting varied from region to region, so while some areas were hit extremely hard, others did not see persecutions at all. Unlike France, however, German lands of the Holy Roman Empire did not have a strong governing body like the Parlement of Paris to curb witchcraft abuses. Add to this fragmentation of authority the legality of torture under Carolina law and folk beliefs that seamlessly integrated with demonology of the day and it becomes apparent why the death count in Germany was around 25,000 people— half of what some scholars estimate as the total number of deaths from all witchcraft persecutions in early modern Europe.

My journey into Bamberg's past began in front of a peach-colored pharmacy. On the corner of Franz-Ludwig-Straße and Promenade-straße, Saint Hedwig Apotheke appears to be your average shop, but the plaque affixed to the outside wall says otherwise. Pictured on a small glass plate is a Renaissance-style building adorned with a statue of Justice and her scales. Within this engraving, a river gently flows by, trees sprout from its banks, and the structure looks almost inviting—almost. One word in the description stands out above the rest: *"Malefizhaus."*

Inside the Bamberg "Witch House" the walls ran with blood. The rooms were cells of solitary confinement, and furniture the strappado, the rack. Screams and forced confessions polluted the air: it was a place of debasement that begat generations of trauma. But for Prince-Bishop Dornheim and suffragan Bishop Förner, the duo driving the Bamberg witch hunts, this was their crowning achievement: a combined prison, courthouse, and torture chamber responsible for holding, trying, and brutalizing citizens charged with witchcraft.

My tour guide through Bamberg's witch history was a witty, thoughtful woman who had spent many years researching the city's dark past. She began by passing around images of early modern German art depicting the witches' sabbath (which naturally included Hans Baldung Grien's work). Then, she offered gruesome detail about the torture devices used at the Malefizhaus like the tongue loosener and the breast ripper—once put into the fire, it would slide into flesh like a hot knife through butter. The guide was quick to draw parallels between the oppressive tactics of witch hunting and other government persecutions of today. She compared the dehumanization and torture in Bamberg to the acts of inhumanity making headlines in the United States that very week, where the government was caging the children of Latinx migrant people in torturous conditions, depriving them of basic human rights. Propaganda is a necessary tool for tyrants, she said, so abusers of power always need the right PR. Drawing another parallel to an even darker moment in her country's history, my tour guide positioned Förner as the Joseph Goebbels to Dornheim's Adolph Hitler.

In the "Witch House of Bamberg" chapter of *Embracing the Darkness*, John Callow outlines how Förner "provided much of the intellectual framework for the subsequent trials" by publishing dozens of his sermons on witchcraft well before the 1626 wave of witch hunting began. Thanks to Martin Luther, the German territories had birthed Protestantism a century before, and it was a growing threat to Catholic strongholds like Bamberg. In light of this, Förner's speeches at the pulpit had been grooming the community to fear the encroaching dangers of Protestantism and other Pagan evils and to stop at nothing to eradicate them. "Förner believed that, in their poverty and misery, the people of Bamberg were turning for succor not to the Roman Catholic Church, but to countless 'cunning women and little women-witches,'" Callow writes, "who would lead the simple, the ill-effected, and the plain weak willed to certain damnation, were they not quickly and effectively controlled."

Förner, like Heinrich Kramer, lay blame on women as the main instigators of witchcraft. And throughout Germany, women did make up about 75–85 percent of accusations and executions. However, the witch hunters in Bamberg widened their scope. Because Dornheim and Förner's hunts overtook the city to such an extent, children and men—powerful men included—were victimized, too. Many individuals lost their lives and their families in the flames, but two stand out. In each case, the printed word would dictate their fate: for one, it was a book; for another, a letter.

Walking from the former site of the Malefizhaus across the quaint old town center, the tour guide led me to the surviving seventeenth-century homes of Bamberg's wealthiest. She pointed up at a particularly nice-looking one, which was supposedly where a boy, Hans Morhaubt, had lived. Recounting his story, she described a quick escalation from reading a forbidden book, to being interrogated by the Hexen-Kommission, to Hans, his family maid, his mother and father, and eventually their neighbors being sent to the stake.

Long before Goethe's Faust climbed the heights of the Brocken, the story of Doctor Faustus traveled through Germany across tavern tables. The legend of this German man who sold his soul to the Devil for the finer things in life was first published in the 1580s, but Bamberg had unique ties to the tale even before that. According to town records, the Bamberg Prince-Bishop paid someone named Dr. Faustus 10 gulden for reading his horoscope in 1520. A century later, Hans Morhaubt would be caught reading *The History of Doctor Johann Faustus* by his Jesuit schoolmaster and, given the book's talk of demons, links to Bamberg, and origins at a Protestant press, it would be the end of the boy and his family.

In Bamberg, torture-driven confessions led directly to the naming of other "witches" in the community—which bred new suspects, more torture, and more deaths. The most famous story that survives from Bamberg's witch hunts, however, is perhaps the only one in the early modern witch hunts that left primary source evidence of what people accused of witchcraft were thinking and feeling throughout the harrowing process.

A year after Johannes Junius's wife was executed for witchcraft, the fifty-five-year-old burgomaster of Bamberg was accused by a local doctor of attending a witches' sabbath in the chamber of the city council. "The accusation was," according to Lara Apps in *Male Witches in Early Modern Europe*, "aimed directly at the top levels of urban society, and would seem to have been as much about civic politics, power and honour as about anything else."

Junius was promptly arrested. As with all suspected witches who entered the Malefizhaus, Junius was stripped of his clothes and his body was searched for the Devil's mark. (This humiliating practice was de rigueur across Europe in early modern witch interrogations.) According-ing to trial records, Junius had a patch of discolored skin that, when pricked, did not bleed or cause him pain, which was considered proof of a demonic pact. There was nothing further he could say to prove his innocence.

After being tortured repeatedly with thumbscrews, leg screws, and the strappado, Junius refused to own up to anything. A week of sadistic punishments continued, during which Junius's shoulders were ripped from their sockets by the strappado and his nail beds pierced and bloodied by thumbscrews. Pushed to the brink, he finally confessed to practicing witchcraft and renouncing God, and then named another government official as a fellow witch. But in a surviving letter Junius wrote to his daughter, we see the mechanisms at work behind his false confession. After what he went through in the Malefizhaus, Junius's admissions were, according to his own words, "sheer lies and inventions."

Stacked in among other papers documenting his trial, the letter was likely spirited away by someone as a final favor. In it, Junius reveals in heartbreaking detail that it was the executioner himself who pleaded with Junius to confess something—anything. "Sir, I beg you, for God's sake confess something, whether it be true or not," the executioner told him. "Invent something, for you cannot endure the torture which you will be put to . . . but one torture will follow after another until you say you are a witch."

Junius's correspondence has been an invaluable resource for those studying the witch hunts in the past few centuries. As Apps explains, his letter has been used "as evidence for the injustice of witch trials; as proof that those accused generally confessed only under duress, espe-cially torture; as proof that those accused of witchcraft, especially during epidemics of witch hunting, did not need to have engaged in any tra-ditional folk practices or 'magic' to be accused of witchcraft and exe-cuted for it; [and, most relevant in Bamberg] as proof that interrogators 'scripted' confessions for the accused and backed up these scripts with the threat of violence and actual violence."

Junius's letter provides invaluable insight into the psyches of those undergoing torture for crimes they did not commit. It is worth emphasizing, however, that the only reason we have such evidence is because Junius was an educated, rich man and had the capability to secret the letter away—let alone the ability to write it. He was given an honorable death—decapitation by sword—before his body was burned at the stake on August 6, 1628.

From the streets where Bamberg's elite lived, it was only a few minutes' walk to the Schönleinsplatz. Now a grassy park with a statue of Prince Regent Luitpold of Bavaria mounted on horseback, this was once the field of the "Black Cross." At the height of the witch hunt, bodies burned day and night, for it was believed they must fully turn to ash or their souls might hang back. The River Regnitz nearly ran black with so much soot. The air was thick with the smoke of human remains. The townspeople began to talk of the stench, of the pain in their lungs. Fearing that popular support might sour against his witch hunting whims, Dornheim—also known as the Hexenbrenner (Witch Burner) and Hexenbischof (Witch Bishop)—moved the site of execution to the neighboring suburb of Zeil am Main, so the people of Bamberg couldn't easily witness the near continuous carnage.

It was the invading Swedish army battling the 30 Years' War that finally brought Dornheim's witch hunt to a halt in 1631. (Förner had died a year before.) By then, about a thousand people had been executed and the community fabric torn asunder. The city would never forget its deadliest witch hunt, though. Zeil am Main now houses a museum dedicated to the hunt, and Bamberg is one of the few places with a scholarly witch hunting tour offered by its official tourism office. Of all people, Germans know nothing good comes from ignoring history.

My tour had ended, but I kept walking through Bamberg, taking in the sights. The half-timbered Old Town Hall is postcard perfect, balanced on a bridge spanning the Regnitz as it has since the fourteenth century. The frescoes on either side come to life in fiery oranges and reds, more Baroque finery to tantalize the eyes and give the impression of a powerful city worthy of your attention, your respect, and perhaps even your submission. This was the same impetus that drove the construction of the Malefizhaus, when it, too, stood as a visual symbol of state power, its great punishing forces only a mirror of God's.

Bamberg is a UNESCO World Heritage Site, which means it represents, among other things, architectural and artistic ingenuity and the apex of human achievement. It is a city people visit to immerse themselves in the "finer things" in life, a place ripe for self-congratulation about humanity's greatest gifts, which usually comes at the cost of ignoring our fatal flaws. But I'd argue that the memorialization of pain and trauma is just as precious—if not more historically meaningful—as any well-preserved city and its priceless works of art and architecture. This pain and trauma are becoming more and more visible in Bamberg, in small memorials laid out across town and in the official witch hunting tours that now run year-round.

As Daniel P. Reynolds explains in *Postcards from Auschwitz: Holocaust Tourism and the Meaning of Remembrance*, tourists have a responsibility when visiting sites where atrocities took place. Bearing witness to these histories means "negotiat[ing] the boundaries between knowledge seeking and voyeurism," Reynolds writes. "The traumatic experiences of victims impose ethical obligations on those who listen to and represent testimony."

I gave much thought to navigating the line between seeker and voyeur with grace as I visited so many places of torture and death. Even though the sites of the witch hunts represent suffering that ended hundreds of years ago—and nothing *nearly* on the scale of the Holocaust

Reynolds writes of—I continually endeavored to resist a cavalier outlook or become immune to suffering.

To talk about witches today—especially as someone who is part of a witchcraft community and who writes and teaches about aspects of historical witch hunting—can be complicated. It is simultaneously speaking in archetypes and of actual people, at once referencing history, myth, politics, and popular culture. There is perverse humor in certain aspects, and unspeakable horror in others. To truly interface with the loaded term *witch* means speaking of the sacred and profane in the same breath, code-switching swiftly from the empiricism of a social scientist to the tactical passion of an activist to the embodied practice of a witch—all the while never fully leaving one identity behind.

"Tourism resists stable forms of identity," Reynolds asserts. "Indeed, some forms of tourism may bring about a profound destabilization of identity."

The witch hunts were also a time of destabilized identities, where a mother, a lover, a brother, a neighbor could shape-shift into the ultimate evil in the blink of an eye. Unconsciously, I found myself shape-shifting in my travels, too. Faced with so many places of suffering and oppression, I lost the taste for self-punishment. It suddenly felt foolish and wasteful not to feast gratefully on the imperfect banquet I've been given. The addiction to self-sabotage I had long held on to finally lifted like the sun clearing summer rain. I uncovered new ways of being and understanding my identity as I toured witch site after witch site, my ears pricking with premonitions and feelings I could not codify as I took on new attributes and discarded parts of myself along the way. Spend enough time immersed in the past, and you may find yourself forced to change the present.

PAGAN PAST AND PAGAN PRESENCE
Kilkenny, Ireland

AT KYTELER'S INN, A BLACK CAT BECKONED. It arched in agitation on a sign above the doorway, at once a welcome and a warning. Inside, a band played "Ring of Fire" as I settled in at the bar. Perfumed gin wafted from a glass in front of me. Football was on the TV. In the walls, on the floor, at the bar, the stone and wood were worn, and it looked like any medieval pub—save for the witch statue in the corner. I sat on a stool taking it all in for over two hours, looking like someone casing the place—or maybe just a lonesome traveler. The gin flowed; I jumped in the river.

Lively Irish accents lilted through the rafters; some fell in a growl at my feet. It was late afternoon on a lazy summer day and people were talking sport, love, and life. Boredom threatened, so I took my drink to the basement to stretch my legs. More a cavern than a room, the Tavern Bar is held up by pillars of Kilkenny marble, some of which date to 1324. Back then this place was owned by a wealthy woman—some say a witch.

Tipping my gin, I finished my umpteenth drink under the moody subterranean lights. I ordered another and ran my hand absentmindedly across one of the pillars, hundreds of years beneath my fingertips. Drink refreshed, I took in the hypnotic scent of juniper—sweet, woody, crisp. Head spinning, I held my glass high, toasting the namesake of the tavern, and through the bottom of my glass I saw Dame Alice. First, she was the hissing of tonic bubbles, the flirtation of ice cubes clinking. Then, she was a face in a pillar, cheekbones muted gray, her waist the curve of stone. I shut my eyes, then opened them. She had fully taken shape.

Other patrons paid no mind. They faded to mere ghosts as a gauzy silence enveloped the room. And then it was the two of us—three if you count the large black cat circling her heels. Dame Alice Kyteler's legend and life story erupted at once from her lips, like two strains of music resonating in harmony, then in discord. It was hard to tell them apart.

The daughter of a Flemish merchant, Alice had wanted for few things in life. She controlled money as a lender, controlled acreage as a landowner, but could not control the gossip about her. She laughed delivering that last line, looking down at the cat who moved about her skirts, hunting loose threads like his life depended on it. A purring companion, a kitchen mouser, a harmless pet—but the cat had been suspect, too.

Alice had had four husbands. When her trials began, she had already buried three, feeling sorrow for some more than others. Suspicious of her motives, Alice's stepchildren began to accuse her of unsavory things. They wondered why their fathers had died so unexpectedly, had been taken ill so suddenly. And most of all there was the question of their inheritance—the *money*. Her eyes glistened with tears, but I couldn't tell if she was laughing at her misfortune or weeping for it.

Alice's stature, her wealth, and her long line of men would be used against her. Kyteler was accused of denying the Christian faith and leading a covert gang of heretical sorcerers in Kilkenny. According to records from the Diocese of Ossory, "over an oaken fire they boiled the intestines and interior organs of cocks sacrificed to demons" along with "certain horrifying worms, various herbs, and also nails of the dead, buttock hairs, and frequently clothes of children who died without baptism, as well as many other abominable ingredients, in a pot made from the head of a certain decapitated thief." Then, Kyteler's alleged sect of witches cooked these "various powders, ointments, and potions, and also candles from greasy fat left in the said pot, as they said various incantations, to arouse love or hatred, to kill and also to afflict the bodies of faithful Christians, and for innumerable other purposes."

But that wasn't all. Alice was accused of poisoning her first three husbands, as well as poisoning her current husband, who remained barely alive, his hair and fingernails all falling out, nearly at death's door. Finally, Alice Kyteler was accused of having sex with an incubus named Robin or Robert. He was said to have known her in ways none of her husbands ever could. He knew the flush of her skin, the arch of her back. He slaked her thirst like no other, they said.

Sometimes, he took the form of a cat.

She was amused, then betrayed by these hostilities—but not surprised. She knew wealth was as deadly an intoxicant as any and how it could easily lead you astray. But it wasn't Alice's stepchildren alone who wanted her quite literally to pay. There was a man of the church, she spat, face pinched into a glower, who was unnaturally obsessed with Kyteler's supposed sins.

In 1317, English bishop Richard Ledrede had come all the way from the papacy—then in Avignon—to become Bishop of Ossory. He was called to instill order to this so-called lawless land, which was then believed by many Catholics from the continent to be Christian on the surface but Pagan underneath. Ledrede's obsession with heretical sorcery—inspired by Pope John XXII's views no doubt—began to stir up superstition in the minds of Kilkenny's citizens, too. It was Ledrede who convened the Inquisitional court made up of knights and nobles to prosecute Alice. In fact, Ledrede pursued Alice so doggedly that he was briefly arrested and imprisoned in Kilkenny Castle by an esteemed relative of hers, Chancellor of Ireland Roger Outlawe: kin to Alice's beloved son William.

Dame Alice stopped mid-sentence to grab a nearby broom and began to sweep the floor of the Tavern Bar. It was beneath her, perhaps, but phantasms have their own proclivities. Her red-gold hair was dancing fire as she stirred ancient dirt from the ground. Swirling the broom in circles, she made the bristles scratch out an earthy symphony. The act was in keeping with another accusation documented in a less-than-trustworthy source, for it was also reported that certain townspeople saw Alice sweeping the streets like this and repeating an incantation after sundown: "To the house of William my sonne, Hie all the wealth of Kilkennie towne."

Alice and the broom twisted across the stone floor, humming. But then she stopped, her hand gripping the handle with purpose as she steadied herself. Her tongue raked slowly across her lips, and I heard the cat's purr begin to grow louder and louder as she let me peer into the past. Alice looked up, and I heard the story—the hearsay—once more.

The bishop's imprisonment did not last long. There was only so much sway the secular Irish authorities—chancellor of Ireland included—had over the all-powerful Catholic Church. Ledrede was eventually freed and doubled down on his desire to see Alice burn. She managed to hold off arrest for as long as she could, but realizing there would be no easy end for her, she used her great means to leave Ireland for England.

Alice never returned to her birthplace, her home. But now, she avowed, she can come and go as she pleases. She can walk—or sweep if the mood strikes—the grounds of her former estate that still lures curious travelers like me here, drawn in by the lore of her name.

I had so many questions, but my vision was blurring and Alice would communicate no more. She stared mutely as I tipped my glass for another drink and vanished as peculiarly as she appeared. The room erupted in chatter, in music. The basement bar was getting more and more crowded, and I needed air—and answers. I paid my tab and went back upstairs and outside, past the statue of Alice, broom in hand and cat at her feet, that stood in a corner near the door.

I stepped out of Kyteler's Inn and onto the medieval thorough-fare. The sun was out, but flagging. Turning left, I cut up a side pas-sage called the "Butter Slip," fossils shining white in black Kilkenny marble beneath my boots. Nearly back on High Street, I walked past a restaurant, Petronella. The place is named after Petronilla de Midia (also known as de Meath), located mere steps away from where she burned alive in Alice's stead.

Furious that a woman—a witch—had escaped justice, Bishop Ledrede forged ahead in his case even after Alice escaped. He arrested multiple other people who found themselves entangled in his web, including Petronilla de Midia, who was reputedly Alice's maid in whom she confided over the years. At Ledrede's direction, Petronilla was repeatedly flogged. In excruciating pain, she passed her breaking point.

Using torture, the bishop obtained Petronilla de Midia's confes-sion and all the information about Kyteler he needed to hear. Petronilla admitted to renouncing God and to practicing demonic magic that Alice Kyteler had taught her, even offering sacrifices to demons and acting as a medium. She also confessed to cleaning up after Kyteler and her demon lover's trysts—and goddess knows what that entailed.

In some accounts of the tale, Alice's home was searched again, and when the authorities looked through her closet, they found "a wafer of sacramental bread, having the devil's name stamped thereon instead of Jesus Christ, and a pipe of ointment wherewith she greased a staff, upon which she ambled and galloped through thick and thin, when and in what manner she listed."

Ointments such as the one described above used for magical flight, or transvection, would become part of the early modern witch-on-a-broomstick discourse centuries later. However, it remains unclear if such a thing was ever found in Alice's home. But flying ointment or no, Petronilla's confession was enough to get her killed. She was burned alive with much fanfare for the whole town there to see. The rest of those Ledrede arrested were given punishments of various penances—nothing more. Petronilla de Midia would go down in history as the first woman to be executed for heresy in Ireland. Nevertheless, it is Alice Kyteler whose name is most remembered.

The history of witch hunting in Ireland isn't as bloody or storied as that of nearby Scotland or England, which is why Dame Alice and her cohorts remain so captivating. Witches didn't stir up nearly the same dread on the Emerald Isle as they did elsewhere.

Ronald Hutton explains in "Witch Hunting in Celtic Societies" that the Irish somehow "managed to absorb a fervent Counter-Reformation Catholicism without also importing the stereotype of demonic witchcraft that commonly accompanied it." And yet, Kyteler's case has notable hallmarks of the early modern witch hunts, foreshadowing their particulars hundreds of years prior.

"Ledrede's prosecution of the Kyteler case offers a classic representation of the witch craze in many of its aspects," asserts Maeve Brigid Callan in *The Templars, the Witch, and the Wild Irish: Vengeance and Heresy in Medieval Ireland*. "An older woman who deviates from the norm is charged with outrageous crimes against God and decency in a deliberate subversion of Christian ritual and patriarchal order."

But unlike most accused witches, Alice was rich. She was educated. She had connections. Nevertheless, there is much about Ledrede's witch hunting that has a familiar ring to it, especially in poor Petronilla de Midia's torture-driven confession, which Callan suggests was "largely shaped by Ledrede," through its volatile combination of "*maleficia* with diabolical sorcery and ritual and love magic with apostasy." Ultimately, it was the Bishop of Ossory and his ideas of heresy and dark magic steeped in fourteenth-century French demonology who spun the accusations of Alice's stepchildren into something far more sinister.

In search of surviving remnants of Kilkenny's medieval witch hunt, I headed down the bustling High Street to Saint Mary's. This thirteenth-century cruciform church was central to the community in Alice's day, and it was the place where her son William Outlawe was confronted with his imposed penances by Bishop Ledrede after she skipped town. Now, the stone structure and its many ornate carvings are preserved as the Medieval Mile Museum, which offers a glimpse into Ireland's past through its treasured artifacts and architecture.

I studied the aging graves outside that mark the final remains of Kilkenny's richest, before confirming the pronunciation of "Kyteler" with the docents inside the museum. (They said Dame Alice's name— unfortunately—rhymes with "Hitler," though I heard other locals say the name with a bit more "eh.") The selection of imposing Celtic crosses had me dreaming up epic tattoos, but Kilkenny Castle awaited, so I moved on to see the end of the Medieval Mile.

Built in the twelfth century, the castle complex resides on a rolling landscape of bright emerald grass—the kind of cat's eye electric green that blankets Ireland. Many elements of the medieval foundation and fortification remain in the castle, and it's easy to imagine Ledrede shut away here in his brief imprisonment. Initially built by the Anglo-Normans, Kilkenny Castle signifies the town's long-running divisions along ethnic lines, between the indigenous Irish and the settlers/ invaders/colonizers from England and beyond.

My final destination was the Kyteler burial slab at Saint Canice's Cathedral on the other side of town. A short walk from Kyteler's Inn lies the divide between what was formerly "English Town" or "High Town" where the merchants and wealthy colonists lived, and "Irish Town," which was decidedly less well off. At the time, Saint Canice's was the religious heart of the latter.

The Round Tower on the site of Saint Canice's is over a thousand years old and one of the few you can still climb all the way to the top. The cathedral itself dates back to 1202 and inside is the black marble slab belonging to Alice's father Joseph Kyteler, inscribed with a simple Flemish cross. The Kyteler slab was found near Alice's home (now Kyteler's Inn) in the late nineteenth century and brought here. Not far from Joseph Kyteler lies his daughter's greatest foe, Bishop Richard Ledrede, who passed away after serving in Ossory for over forty years.

An effigy chiseled out of stone is affixed to Ledrede's tomb, depicting the bishop wearing a traditional robe and sandals—a reference to his humble beginnings as a priest in the Franciscan order. But despite his path, there is evidence that points to Ledrede being quite transfixed by the almighty dollar.

Maeve Brigid Callan cites a letter from the King of England and Lord of Ireland Edward III to Pope Innocent VI that is not so complimentary toward the Bishop of Ossory. It says that "'forgetful of his original mendicancy,' Ledrede fabricated heresy charges in order to extort money from the accused." Callan adds that the "allegation can be substantiated by William Outlaw's payment to the bishop of £1,000 shortly after being released from prison and perhaps explains his enthusiasm in his prosecution of William's mother, an exceptionally wealthy woman."

Greed was indeed a motivation in many early modern witch hunts, as the church, state, and/or powerful individuals often had the motives and ability to swallow up possessions of the accused and convicted. Once again, the case of Alice Kyteler foreshadows much of what would occur in witch hunts across Scotland, England, and continental Europe.

Taking in the church's aging finery, I caught a face staring back at me from one of the columns. I moved closer to confirm my suspicions. No, it wasn't Alice, but the Green Man, his marble mouth bursting with leafy foliage. This spirit or symbol of vegetative renewal was important enough to the indigenous Irish 800 years ago that it was built into the structure of this Christian church. Today, the Green Man remains an important symbol of nature's potency for contemporary Pagans and witches in Ireland and beyond. It made me think of the zodiac in San Miniato al Monte in Florence and of the ways Pagan nature-worship has been both incorporated and rejected by Christianity over the past millennium.

When I walked back to my hotel in the brisk summer twilight, music burst from the open doors of every pub on High Street. I pulled my jacket tightly around me like a protective shroud. Crossing the bridge by Kilkenny Castle, I saw the ramparts reflected in the River Nore, a watery inversion of its earthly glory. It was a beautiful but distorted vision of a reality just out of reach, much like the Pagan past so many of us who practice witchcraft try to apprehend.

In "The Nearest Kin of the Moon: Irish Pagan Witchcraft, Magic(k) and the Celtic Twilight," Jenny Butler writes about the appeal of uniquely Irish witch figures like the "cunning woman" called the *bean feasa* and her male equivalent the "fairy doctor" to contemporary Irish witches and Pagans.

"It must be noted that many of the connections being made by Pagan witches with traditional healers, and the practice of certain types of rituals, involve some reinterpretations and reimagining of the past,"

Butler explains. As with much contemporary witchcraft in Ireland and beyond, there is often a flexible understanding of history at play when practitioners seek to ground their workings in bygone eras. "Historicity becomes ancillary when more imaginative connections are being made between present and past spiritualities and context can at times be transcended in favor of making 'magical' connections explicit," Butler continues. She adds that whether these connections are "true" or "false" is often the least compelling piece of the puzzle to explore.

The deeply romantic notion of a Pagan witchcraft practice that survived unchanged from pre-Christian times is not historically verifiable. But the lack of evidence for a witch cult doesn't preclude a magical dialogue between past and present that can exist within your own practice, within your own ancestry.

Staring at the reflection of the castle in a sheen of black water, I thought of the Green Man's carved face in Saint Canice's Cathedral. Though softened by time, it was a startling reminder that what came before can persist against all odds. The leaves that sprout from the Green Man's mouth proclaim the all-consuming power of nature, to which we all must ultimately submit, regardless of belief.

SOWING SEEDS, ALTERED STATES
London, England

THE OCCULT IS INSEPARABLE FROM the landscape of London. Aged, ornate buildings, churches, and monuments bear visible links to ancient mythology and secret societies. Symbols scratched into walls and containers filled with nails, urine, human hair, and other ephemera to ward off malicious magic—"witch marks" and "witch bottles"—are still unearthed during routine renovations. Esoteric iconoclasts are memorialized by plaques and numerous walking tours around town. There are even faux hieroglyphs at Harrods.

Compared to the puritanical avoidance of anything Pagan in the US, it's a breath of fresh air to land in Heathrow and take the Underground directly to an occult destination. Within a single mile radius is the Atlantis Bookshop, where modern Wicca bloomed in the basement; the British Museum, a haven for ancient artifacts that shaped conceptions of the witch; Treadwell's Books, where esotericism and feminism commingle on the shelves; and the Mandrake, what *Fodor's Travel* calls "the most mysteriously magical hotel in all of London." I couldn't help but stay.

The Mandrake's namesake is *Mandragora officinarum*, a plant with many medicinal and magical tricks up its hoary sleeves. Legend has it that the mandrake root—with its uncanny, humanlike shape—will scream when pulled up out of the ground and immediately kill the culprit. In witchcraft practices, this peculiar perennial "is a powerful example of where a plant's actual spirit is directly invoked in order to get results," discloses Corinne Boyer in *Plants of the Devil*. "It is one of the very few plants where its historical magical use has survived into modern times."

Golden, dagger-spiked leaves fan out around a watchful eye above the Mandrake's entrance. I walked past the shadows of shapes cast on the floor leading up to a sacred geometry skull mural. Inside the lobby, the lighting is dim, the decor animalistic and opulent. Doors blend interiors into hidden enclaves for ritual and revelry. It's a heathen feast for the senses.

Upon reaching my room, I was greeted by a panorama of jasmine and passion flowers out on the terrace framed by burgundy, tiger-striped curtains. Mixed into the usual hotel materials, I spied a menu for the Mandrake's "Spiritual Wellbeing Concierge Service," which offers an array of syncretic, witchy experiences for guests. The hotel espouses the belief that "hedonism and spirituality should live side by side to inspire, to tantalise, and to heal." They had my attention.

That night, I signed up for one of the Mandrake's programs combining elements of breathwork, meditation, and ancestor veneration. Not sure what to expect, I arrived at the hotel's basement club-cum-healing space in my cheerful New York City uniform of black monochrome. Before the opening ritual, some of the participants shared life-changing experiences they had had at prior events led by the leader of the workshop. They chatted gamely with one another as I sat quietly in the corner, reapplying my fuchsia lipstick with a shaky hand. (Naturally, I wanted to look my best for my lineage.)

The facilitator began with a discussion of Samhain as the witches' New Year and a time to shed old skins and honor the dead. Then, in front of an altar piled high with pumpkins and squashes, I lay down in the dark surrounded by a dozen strangers. Breathing in and out in unison, I could hear the rasp of deep inhalations and exhalations around me. Some sounded pained, cathartic; others blissful. Ever wary of falling into spiritual dilettantism or appropriation territory, I was pleasantly surprised at how the evening played out.

The guide led us deeper into ourselves. She asked us to thank those who came before and fixate on what guidance we might need from our lineage. She asked what we could, in turn, offer our ancestors. Which parts of them within us did we cherish; which parts did we need to destroy? My eyes were closed, but streaks of violet coursed through my line of sight. A phrase, a fragment, slipped into my mind:

The things you're carrying may not be your own.
The things you're carrying may not be your own.
The things you're carrying may not be your own.

I imagined my bloodline flowing slow and lavalike underground. It burned across continents, simmered through centuries, splitting, forking, coursing in all directions. So much of my lineage is completely foreign, lives I cannot fathom no matter how hard I try—but there can still be family in the unfamiliar. Lying on my back, I continued to breathe, thanking those who came before, who led me to this body, this city, this work. I listened in anticipation, waiting for what I don't know. My mind was reeling; limbs electric. Every exhale was a purge, every inhale a balm. The channel was open and knowing washed over me in a wave.

Two hours collapsed into minutes. I was in a completely different place and time when our guide interrupted me mid-thought to gently lead us into the present. Bodies stirred and came back to life. I was in a room full of strangers in a hotel basement again. We were asked to open up about our experiences if we felt called to. I was at a loss for words. My journey thus far had proven to be both an induction and a return, but I had much further to go before I could share.

Already coaxing open the doors of perception, the Mandrake was living up to its reputation. Traveling itself is an altered state, and I wanted to prolong my trip. With my mind on the magic of the hotel's feral namesake, full immersion into plant lore beckoned. I wanted to walk on fertile ground, to interface with flora foundational to the legacy of the witch. The oldest botanical garden in the city, Chelsea Physic Garden, was just the place.

Founded by the Worshipful Society of Apothecaries in 1673—decades before witch hunts went not-so-gently into that good night—Chelsea Physic Garden was built for apothecaries to teach their apprentices about the healing and harming powers of plants. Tucked away in the former village of Chelsea right off the Thames, the garden has been blessed by a microclimate. The air is warmer, the soil richer than other parts of London. Since the site was deemed worthy of planting some 350 years ago, it has housed species from around the world.

Walking through a small arch in the high brick walls that enclose the place is like entering a temple of sorts. Although the garden was created by men, it is plants that rule inside. Small signs denote poisonous plants that should not be touched. Others indicate healing plants that could save your life. Still others mark plants that offer the raw materials for clothing and furniture—and then there are those whose beauty is their bounty. There's a sense of veneration in the Chelsea Physic Garden. Inside this green cathedral the incense is oxygen-rich air, the steeple a verdant canopy, the stained glass a collage of petals, the holy order botanists, birds, and insects quietly buzzing about, tending with reverence to the plant life as they have done for centuries.

The garden continues its tradition as a center for learning. A grade-school group of curious kids was winding through as I took in the Garden of Useful Plants, the Garden of Edible Plants, and the Garden of Medicinal Plants. Voices automatically lower to a hush when in the garden, as if everyone else feels it is a sacred place, too. A friendly orange moggy appeared out of a flower bed and stopped to slide her shaggy feline mass across my legs before ducking back into the brush. Around me a wealth of information blossomed from signage between the stalks. There are sections dedicated to species from every corner of the world: you can find yourself in Asia, the Middle East, or the Americas, but it is in the British Isles where witches make themselves known.

"While the British flora contains only 1,600 species, up to a quarter are said to have medicinal uses," a plaque reads, citing the Druids and the Romans as the early keepers of plant knowledge before it became the province of the Christian church. It wasn't the church alone that took responsibility for plant knowledge, though. There were also folk healers whose familiarity with magical and medicinal plant remedies made them indispensable to their communities—for the most part. "The 15th-17th centuries saw folk healing driven underground as many women healers were persecuted as witches," the sign continues.

In the British Isles, folk healers, often called cunning folk, were part of a distinct magico-medical stratum. "Cunning folk . . . always dealt with a nameless art that addressed various aspects of medicine, magic, and divination" writes Nigel Pennick in *Witchcraft & Secret Societies of Rural England.* They could aid you in exorcisms or contacting the dead, healing a sick animal or family member, finding a lost or stolen item, and conjuring a beloved to suit your fancy. "The powers of the cunning folk are ambiguous," Pennick continues, "useful for life and healing, but also for illicit private gain and harm. The practitioner elicits both admiration and fear among those with whom he or she has business."

Recent discoveries have shed new light on the ways of the cunning folk. One seventeenth-century London cunning man's book of charms, conjurations, and prayers has been made available to the general public. *The Grimoire of Arthur Gauntlet* isn't just a single man's knowledge, though, but draws from the magical and medical skill sets of other practitioners—both men and women—whom he encountered and worked alongside. Compiled between 1614 and 1636, the grimoire lists spells and cures that require a variety of plants I came across in the garden: valerian, apple, henbane, poppy.

"Write in an Apple Reguell Lucifer Sathanus And say I conjure thee Apple by these three names written in thee That whosoever shall eat thee may burn in my love until such time she hath fulfilled my desire," Gauntlet's grimoire instructs. He also offers herbal remedies for common ailments, divinatory spells to contact angels, and recipes for perfumes one can create for devotional or practical purposes.

As my walk continued, I found witches lurking in more seedbeds. The sign for *Stachys officinalis* (sometimes known as common hedge nettle or wood betony) announces that the plant "preserves the liver and the bodies of men from the danger of epidemical diseases and from witchcraft." This knowledge is attributed to botanist, herbalist, physician, and astrologer Nicholas Culpepper, the man who wrote *The Complete Herbal* in 1653. Culpepper's work was widely consulted by cunning folk and makes multiple mentions of witchcraft. Other plants he prescribes to repel witches include branches of holly or branches of mistletoe hung around the neck. (Gauntlet's grimoire suggests carrying a pomegranate around to ward off witchcraft.)

Although cunning folk are intimately linked to the witch archetype, persecution of folk healers during the witch hunts—despite what the sign in the Physic Garden says—remains a subject of debate. "For many early modern theologians and intellectuals, cunning folk were considered as bad as or even worse than witches," explain Owen Davies and Lisa Tallis in *Cunning Folk: An Introductory Bibliography*. "However, since by and large the common people saw cunning folk as important allies in the struggle against witches and misfortune, they rarely sought to prosecute them for what they practiced." Exceptions do exist, and you'll see cunning women and men deemed witches in witchcraft pamphlets and trial records alike. We also know that English lawmakers were not fond of folk healers, and "it was the concern over those who practiced theft magic, love magic and treasure hunting, rather than witches as they came to be defined later in the century, which led to the first so-called Witchcraft Act of 1542," Davies writes in *Cunning-folk: Popular Magic in English History*. James I's Witchcraft Act of 1604 was directed at both cunning folk and witches, too.

Folk healers, cunning women, or wise women may not have been a driving force of the English witch hunts, but they do occupy a very special place in English magical history. In fact, the first commercial tourist destination in England was Mother Shipton's cave in Knaresborough, Yorkshire, established as a site to be seen by 1630. "Mother" was a common title given to wise women, and Mother Shipton, born Ursula Southeil in a cave by the River Nidd around the year 1488, was the most notorious prophetess—England's Nostradamus she's been called—to ever charm her way across the British Isles.

Much of her biography and words have been fabricated, and many wonder if she was even a real person at all, but there is evidence that the "Witch of Yorkshire" did offer remedies to everyday folk while she was dropping prophesies on the side. Mother Shipton supposedly foresaw the English Civil War, the Great Fire of London, and perhaps even digital connectivity with the couplet: "Around the world thoughts shall fly / In the twinkling of an eye."

Before I headed back to the Mandrake, I stopped at the place where the mandragora grew. There wasn't much to see as the seeds lay dormant, but mere steps away the *Mandragora officinarum* is pictured in a 1597 illustration from *Gerard's Herball*. The plant's roots are split in two, and it looks as if it might walk right off the sign. A creature with a will of its own, just as folklore would portend.

These "visionary nightshades" hold special power, Daniel A. Schulke reveals in *Veneficium: Magic, Witchcraft and the Poison Path*. Plants like mandrake, henbane, belladonna, and thorn apple have "ancient histories of magical use, and [are] characterized by demoniac visions at shamanic doses." They can be spiritually sustaining, and they can be deadly, much like the practice of witchcraft itself.

"The Devil's arsenal includes a specific handful of toxic plants, many of them in the Solanaceae family," explains Corinne Boyer. "The triple nature of these 'Witching Herbs' lie[s] in their ability to heal, harm and facilitate magico-visionary experiences, all outcomes dependent on dosage."

Said to hail from the realm of the Devil, mandrake, henbane, belladonna, and thorn apple are also frequently mentioned in extant writings about the witches' flying ointment, a potent blend of lore where sexuality, spirituality, and hallucinogenics meet. Such magico-sexual connections made even more sense when I thought of my hotel's ethos of uniting spirituality and hedonism as one. The mandrake plant was often called for in spells conjuring "increased fertility, sexual vigour, and attracting a sexual consort," notes Schulke. (And it's no coincidence that the root looks a bit like human genitals, too.)

Leaving the Physic Garden, I reflected on the flora responsible for so much of our sustenance and suffering. These days, plants aren't viewed with much reverence by the general public. They are raw materials to exploit, *things* to be used. But a trip around London's oldest garden will have you sorted. The Chelsea Physic Garden endows visitors with a healthy respect for the power of plant life. (Croplifters Will Be Propagated, warns a sign inside.)

Walking back into a world of concrete and bleating cars was leaving an Edenic paradise. But there was something else I needed to see. Like Eve, I was enrapt by a certain tree intimately tied to great suffering. I had to press on beyond the garden's borders to satisfy my curiosity.

Between the twelfth and eighteenth centuries, Tyburn was the place for public executions. Little is left of the gallows where many convicted witches were hanged in London save for a cement traffic triangle in the northeast corner of Hyde Park near the Marble Arch. Fountains spurt across the street, and traffic zips by on all three sides. No one seemed to pay any mind to the unassuming marker I stood staring at when I arrived from the Physic Garden. A small circular plaque marks the location of the Tyburn Gallows. It reads: "The site of Tyburn Tree."

London's witch hunts may not be as famous as those that tore apart Lancashire or East Anglia, but they were certainly just as grim. For so many women and men, the gateway between this world and the next was Tyburn. All who heard tales of this deadly tree gained a healthy sense of respect for it, much like those who knew of the *Mandragora officinarum* and its poisonous brethren. Mother Nature has always had her canny ways to create and destroy, but mankind has been a quick study.

For 600 years, Tyburn Tree saw some 50,000 to 60,000 people meet a grisly end. The gallows there were a triptych of wood beams originally sourced from the elms near Tyburn Brook, and the scaffold that was continually built and rebuilt could hang up to twenty-four people at a time.

According to Matthew Beaumont's account in *Nightwalking: A Nocturnal History of London*, at midnight before a hanging was to take place the following day, a "hanging fair" occurred, and "the bellman of St Sepulchre-without-Newgate recited verses to the men and women who were due to be executed. 'All you that in the condemn'd Holds do lie, / Prepare you, for to Morrow you shall die', he began . . ." A staggering 50,000 to 100,000 people could be in attendance for an execution. Spectators arrived en masse, squeezing together, standing on ladders, elbowing their way through to the grandstand to take in the show. There was no single kind of criminal these gawkers came to see, but the hanging of accused witches no doubt had its own morbidly unique appeal.

In 1585, Margaret Hackett, a sixty-year-old widow, was hanged at Tyburn for allegedly murdering a man through witchcraft.

In 1599, Anne Kirk, another destitute widow, was hanged at Tyburn for allegedly cursing and killing children through witchcraft.

In 1621, Elizabeth Sawyer, a surly woman who confessed to having a canine familiar, was hanged at Tyburn for allegedly practicing witchcraft.

In 1652, Joan Peterson, a London cunning woman, was hanged at Tyburn for allegedly bewitching a client.

It is not possible to fathom every single death of the thousands who died at Tyburn, or who perished in the European witch hunts—or in any mass extinguishing of human life. But that doesn't mean it is pointless to try to keep memories of these people alive.

"Remembering *is* an ethical act. . . . Memory is, achingly, the only relation we can have with the dead," Susan Sontag opines in *Regarding the Pain of Others*. "But history gives contradictory signals about the value of remembering in the much longer span of a collective history."

Western patriarchy has long decided whom we should remember and whom we should forget. But that stranglehold grip is loosening.

Histories are being recovered and rewritten. When it comes to the witch hunts, the past is by no means immutable. Within the last decade, new witch hunt memorials have been proposed or unveiled in Lancaster, Colchester, Kinross, Orkney, Fife, and beyond. Communities are petitioning for posthumous pardons. Historians are digging into records to dispel myths and share long-lost stories. Across the United Kingdom, memories are surfacing, and once-muted voices are now being heard.

THE GHOSTS OF MALKIN TOWER
Lancashire, England

As I traveled north to the home of the Pendle witches, London's humid chill turned sharper, the wind slicing through my thin denim jacket with a frigid sting. I stopped in Nottingham to visit a witchcraft exhibition featuring artifacts from Cornwall's exceptional Museum of Witchcraft and Magic. I was immediately drawn to a jolly ceramic face peering at me from a seventeenth-century witch bottle, just like the ones found all across England in the eaves and walls of homes in cities and rural towns, offering protection from malefic magic. Before heading on, I took a detour through the very real Sherwood Forest of mythical Robin Hood fame, where apotropaic witch marks had recently been uncovered in a nearby cave.

Hiking through the damp woods I was alone with the fog of my breath. My destination was the Major Oak, a tree some 800 years old with hollow enclaves in its trunk perfect for hiding goods—or enchanted beings. I yearned to press my face into its hallowed bark— as I did with the Oak of the Witches in Italy—but the tree has been cordoned off for decades now to keep it alive. I stared at its knotty curves through sheets of November rain before trekking back down the trail, thinking of Robin Hood and his Merry Men stashing treasure in its folds years ago. One reading of the medieval tale actually positions Robin as the Green Man, the deity who embodies the fertile cycles of plant life. There are few English legends that aren't infused with Pagan lore.

On the train once more, I watched the topography continue to transform. Flat fields turned hilly; sheep began to pop up in pastures between small clusters of homes. After hours of travel, I finally arrived in Accrington for the main event: a Pendle witch–themed ghost hunt. Veering between raging rationalist and true-blue believer, I was ready for anything. The evening began with a woman in period costume, teeth blackened, dress ragged, who set the stage for a weekend of ghosts, witches, and history. Then came the table tipping, Ouija sessions, and spirit summoning inside a 700-year-old country manor. The place was reportedly haunted, and each room creaked and groaned with age in ways that would make your skin crawl—but you could order stone-baked pizza from room service twenty-four hours a day. I wondered what the ghosts thought of that.

Before I knew it, it was midnight and we were outside on Pendle Hill. A near-full moon hung in a gauzy sky, and I could feel it wasn't far off from freezing. Two dozen people stood in a circle, hoping to connect with the entities or energies of the Pendle witch trials that might still be in this barren landscape. The only lights were in the distance; everyone turned off their phones and flashlights. Varying degrees of skepticism coursed through each one of us, but curiosity remained our North Star.

The wreckage of Malkin Tower, where one clan of cunning folk once dwelled, was supposedly beneath our feet. The crude limestone hovel where matriarch Elizabeth Southerns and her family eked out a living in the early 1600s isn't standing, but there are foundation stones still stuck in the earth that catch the soles of your shoes and throw you off balance if you aren't careful.

A few people in the party got out a spirit board and began to ask questions. With their hands on the planchette, they asked if anyone or anything could hear them. The wind was keening, and I jogged in place for a few minutes to keep feeling my feet. Some of us watched, faces numb, eyes tearing, and others rested fingers lightly on the small arrow-shaped piece of plastic as it unexpectedly jerked over to the word "Yes."

In the dark, it's easy to see things that aren't there. Hoods and hats obscured the heads and faces of those in the circle, and everyone began to look a bit more sinister. Perception blurred. Someone asked if this entity making contact was someone from Malkin Tower accused of witchcraft.

The pointer slid back to the left.

"Yes," again.

Instead of a friendly ghost hunt, the ritual started to seem a bit more like the godless gathering magistrate Roger Nowell believed occurred here on Good Friday in 1612. Bodies became unwieldly obelisks in the night. Faces were indistinguishable. Bushes on the hill shivered in the wind behind us, and every few minutes a new shadow bloomed where it shouldn't. The leader of the group followed up quickly, asking if the entity making contact was "*actually* a witch."

"Yes."

The crisp night air thickened. It turned smoky on my tongue. The limestone that was underfoot began to transmute into a tall chimney above my head. The figures around me disappeared into phantasmagoric walls. I coughed and waved the acrid clouds from my face, and my eyes began to adjust to the dark. A pot boiled on a fire. A figure slumped against the wall. Second sight revealed an elderly woman, spine a crescent moon. She had no face, just a smoky skein unraveling into nothing but her gnarled fingers meditatively stripping burgundy buds from their stalks, placing them in a pile.

Great burnet she conveyed, somehow, without speaking, for rash and boils and menstrual flow that will not slow. From the Forest of Pendle it grows thick and wild. She sells it to any woman with child so she might survive a bloody birth.

On the ground lay another bouquet of tiny white flowers, petals delicate and sweet, small faces pointing all directions. *Eyebright*. It does as it sounds, she says, somehow still without words. It is for fixing all the ways we do and do not see.

Next to that pile were more greens, small stalks projecting skyward from their leaves, like a snake's forked appendage daring you to pull it up by the root: *Adder's-tongue ferns*. A cooling herb for the skin, and a way to ward off the unnecessary wagging of human tongues—a gossip remedy—she informs.

She kept separating the flowers and the leaves and stalks. Smoke poured from the pot in the center of the room. It began to pop and hiss a prayer.

Upon Good Friday I will fast while I may,
Until I hear them knell
Our Lord's own bell . . .
What hath he in his hand?
Light in leath wand.

The words echoed inside my chest cavity, yet the small room was silent. Still, no face but smoke and black. And then more forms without faces appeared. Worn thin with age and poverty—even the young ones. The crone's body rocked with incantation. Each word well-worn, slipping from her mind from a time before the last abbot swung. My heart was pounding.

What hath he in his other hand?
Heaven's door key.
Open, open heaven door-keys;
Stick, stick, hell door.

Exalting her God, she lets me know their ways. Sometimes, they craft remedies, sell solutions, heal animals. Other times, they beg. In the forest and in the one-room home she shares with her daughter and daughter's children, there are others too: a black dog, a hare, a cat. As isolated as they live, they are never alone. But nearby, there are those who wish them ill or worse.

A cross of blue and another of red

The prayer continued on.

Upon the ground of holy weep

No spell would foretell how the end would unfold. Her clay pictures stuck with hair and teeth became the dungeon that dragged her deep into the silent ground.

Sleepst thou, wakst thou, Gabriel?
No, Lord, I am stayed with stick and stake
That I can neither sleep nor wake.

And there, the prayer abruptly stopped. I looked around the room and the walls were grass, the roof was sky. There was no old woman, no scent of earth and herbs and boiling bones. The group was still asking the spirit board questions. Where had the witch gone? They wanted answers.

A few eager ghost hunters continued to inquire about the gender of any spirits nearby, as if such a thing could really matter in whatever realm they might exist in now. I was too cold to care anymore and began the hike back down the hill to the approaching bus. I took one last look up at the black curves of rock and grass before me. There were no witches here—at least, not anymore.

In the early 1600s, Lancashire was an untamed land thought to be crawling with deviants—"a dark corner of superstition, witchcraft, and popery," as Philip C. Almond puts it in *The Lancashire Witches: A Chronicle of Sorcery and Death on Pendle Hill.* These days, its rolling hills hardly seem untamed. The serene, undulating landscape is broken up by old stone pasture walls, and sheep graze on the same grounds they have for centuries, austere cottages standing here and there.

Between ghost hunts, I boarded a coach through the Pendle countryside to see the area for myself. Famed local tour guide Simon Entwistle was aboard, recounting Lancashire's haunting past with gusto, gesturing out the windows to the passing scenery to punctuate his tale. Ahead, Pendle Hill was an ominous loaf of brown bread, rising in the distance.

What the Salem witch trials are to America, the Pendle witch trials are to England. At the time they occurred in 1612, there had never been so many accused witches tried at one court of assize. The story circulated widely in part because its fantastic particulars were documented so thoroughly by associate clerk Thomas Potts in the 1613 publication, *The Wonderfull Discoverie of Witches in the Countie of Lancaster.*

Like many witch trials, the story in Pendle is one of poverty and power, religion and rivalry. The incident was a result of intercommunity conflict exacerbated by lawmen looking to curry favor with King James I, the only monarch so obsessed with witchcraft he wrote a book of demonology himself.

A single incident sparked the Pendle witch trials, but trouble had already been brewing between the matriarchs of two destitute families: Elizabeth Southerns (Demdike) and Anne Whittle (Chattox)—both cunning women. The former lived with her family in a one-room hovel in the forest of Pendle Hill called Malkin Tower. (At the time, *malkin* was a term meaning "slattern" or "slut.") The latter lived not far away from Demdike's clan on a meager tenant farm. Both families relied on begging, odd jobs, and folk magic to get by.

In March of 1612, Alizon Device, granddaughter of Demdike, passed John Law, an itinerant peddler, and begged from him some pins. He refused, she cursed his lack of generosity, and soon after he fell to the ground, paralyzed. According to Law, an eldritch dog appeared once he had denied Device her request, and everything went black. According to Alizon, it was a familiar spirit she had met before in the shape of a dog. It asked Alizon if it should lame Law, to which she replied: "lame him."

We continued to drive past herds of animals, stone houses stacked side by side, and a misty spread of green all around. Street signs sporting a flying witch began to appear before the bus finally pulled into the Pendle Heritage Center. Inside the historic building is an exhibition about the area's culture of the past thousand years. Apparently, Christianity did not take hold in Lancashire until the seventh or eighth century. From there, a Catholic community built up around Sawley Abbey, which once stood near Pendle Hill until it was forcibly abandoned at the behest of Anglican authorities in the sixteenth century. This shifting spiritual landscape of Pagan-cum-Catholic-cum-Protestant is inseparable from the story of the Pendle witches.

After the altercation with Alizon, John Law collapsed at a nearby alehouse. Word got out to his son about what had happened, so Abraham Law found Alizon and brought her to see his ailing father, who could barely speak, walk, or see. Confronted with Alizon's presence again, John Law accused her of bewitching him. She admitted to harming Law before begging his forgiveness for what she had done. The picture of Christian piety, Law forgave her, but his son was furious and decided to involve the authorities. It was then that magistrate Roger Nowell began to interrogate Alizon about the ordeal.

Unlike the brutal interrogations that occurred in Bamberg at the Malefizhaus, where suspects were subject to inhumane physical abuses to extract confessions, torture required a special warrant and was not a usual part of the witch trial process under English common law. Still, someone like Nowell would know how to wheedle out exactly what he wanted to hear. And what Alizon told him pricked his curiosities: not only was she from a line of cunning women, but she had an animal familiar, too.

Animal familiars were a distinctive feature of English witchcraft, first recorded in the Chelmsford witch trials of 1566. (A sly spotted cat named Satan was at the heart of that affair.) Although European demons and witches were believed to at times appear as animals, the familiar-as-beastly-assistant is uniquely English.

"Familiars were minor demonic spirits that took the shapes of cats and other animals and were believed to assist witches in performing their malevolent magic," writes Brian P. Levack in *The Witchcraft Source-book*. "The familiar likely evolved out of ritual magic practices of centuries past," Levack elaborates, when "educated magicians claimed to be able to imprison imps in bottles or rings and then command them to perform magic."

Nowell began to interrogate the other members of Alizon's family she had implicated in her confession. They *all* admitted to having their own animal familiars. Alizon's grandmother Demdike had a familiar named Tibb, who appeared to her alternately as a black cat, a brown dog, a boy, and a hare. She told Nowell that said spirit once snuck up and suckled blood from under her arm while she was sleeping before she could stop it. Demdike's daughter and Alizon's mother Elizabeth

Device confessed to having a familiar, too, who she said appeared as a brown dog called Ball. Elizabeth's son James also had a familiar who took the shape of a brown—or black—dog named Dandy. And, finally, there was Alizon, who, as Thomas Potts reports, said that she had been visited by something that was a dog, but not a dog. It said it wanted her soul, and if she would let it suckle at her breast, it would in turn "give her power to doe any thing she would."

The relationship between a sorceress and her animal aid was indeed powerful, but it wasn't unconditional. "Witches paid a price for their familiars," affirms Almond. In return for demonic favors they required a feast of bread, milk, animal flesh, or the blood of the witch herself. "Thus the European Devil's mark was supplemented in England by the witch's mark—a super-numerary nipple or teat by which the English witch fed her familiars," Almond explains, proposing a shift from the continental sex pacts to the fiendish fluid bonding of Great Britain. "Where European witches were demonic lovers, English witches were demonic mothers," he writes, "or perhaps, rather, in the English context, the sexual, the maternal, and the demonic were complexly interwoven."

As we've seen, familial bonds weren't always sacrosanct when it came to witchcraft confessions—especially not in Pendle. Alizon blamed her grandmother for facilitating the initial meeting with her canine familiar and suggested Demdike had bewitched a cow and a child to death. Alizon's brother would affirm their grandmother was a malevolent witch as well. Eventually, Alizon's little sister Jennet would blame their mother Elizabeth for organizing the devious doings that went on at the Malkin Tower meeting on Good Friday.

My tour continued through Colne, Barrowford, Newchurch, and Roughlee. We lunched at the Pendle Inn on fish-and-chips and local greens (the restaurant's sign features a high-flying witch). We shopped at Witches Galore, an establishment with all sorts of witchy merch.

And then we made our way to Clitheroe Castle, where I saw the first of the Lancashire Witches Walk memorials. Ten white markers were installed on a fifty-one-mile footpath for the 400th anniversary of the trials in 2012, each one featuring a stanza from a poem about the Pendle witches by Britain's former poet laureate Carol Ann Duffy.

To Roger Nowell and Thomas Potts, the Device family was bad, through and through, but they weren't the only witches in town. It was during Demdike's questioning that she affirmed the wickedness of a rival cunning woman, Chattox, whose daughter, Anne Redfearne, also plied the trade. Demdike said she saw Chattox and her daughter making three "clay pictures" or figures for image magic intended to harm three local individuals. (James Device also confirmed as much, saying Chattox made the figures with the teeth and bones of the dead, stolen from what is now Saint Mary's graveyard at Newchurch.) When interrogated about her workings, Chattox confessed to having a familiar, but said that it was Demdike who had long ago "seduced" her into becoming "subject unto that devilish abominable profession of witchcraft."

The more these poor women of Pendle spoke, the more damning evidence they revealed about each other. It seemed as if all of them had used witchcraft to harm someone in their community.

Accusations of witchcraft between women were quite common in England and beyond, which some scholars have offered as an indication that sexism was not a driving force in the witch hunts. However, most contemporary gender theorists concur that patriarchy as a system is regulated and reified by the misogyny of men *and* the internalized misogyny of women. Within this sexist system, women are socialized to pit themselves against other women for survival.

In "Patriarchal Reconstruction and Witch Hunting" Marianne Hester argues that patriarchy was indeed a significant factor in the witch hunts. "At a local level, use of witchcraft can be seen as a part of the day to day activities of the 'women's community' but—crucially—relying on wider patriarchal gendered notions of the witch, and elite ideas about the unruliness of women and the need to control them," Hester writes. Accusations of witchcraft between women therefore "linked to and served to reinforce—or reconstruct—the male status quo."

In Pendle, women did viciously accuse other women of real and imagined offenses, but it's crucial to remember that men were in charge of every level of persecution and prosecution—as they were in every case of witch hunting in the early modern era. Men like magistrate Nowell were primed to profit off impoverished, uneducated women like Demdike, Device, and Chattox turning against one another, but it was the confession of young Jennet Device that finally put the Pendle case on a fast track to trial.

A girl of about nine according to Potts's telling, Jennet was questioned after Nowell learned of a meeting that occurred at Malkin Tower on Good Friday, organized by Jennet's mother Elizabeth. Jennet's sister Alizon was already in jail by then, and Jennet confessed that her mother invited friends and neighbors—mostly women—to a banquet of beef, bacon, and mutton for a so-called "Christening of the spirit" of Alizon's familiar.

What exactly this meant remains a subject of debate, as naming familiars was not a common practice recorded in the English witch trials. However, James Device admitted that this demonic christening was planned—adding that those present at Malkin Tower also conceived of a plot to blow up Lancaster Castle and rescue those imprisoned there. This was a few years after Catholic vigilante Guy Fawkes had hatched his unsuccessful Gunpowder Plot to assassinate King James, so the threat—no matter how implausible—was not taken lightly. When the authorities searched Malkin Tower, they found clay images buried in the ground that were stuck with human teeth, further confirming the Devices' home as an unholy seat of murderous witchcraft.

At this point, both the Chattox and Device clans were in custody, and Jennet Device transformed into the star witness. She was wielded by Nowell with grace in the courtroom, pointing out each person present who had been at the Malkin Tower meeting. To add insult to injury, Jennet revealed that her mother had taught her two prayers, both seemingly drawn from Catholic liturgies: one to get ale and another to cure the bewitched. The Protestant court was horrified at this syncretic jumble of Catholic witchcraft—just as horrified as Elizabeth Device was that her own child was testifying against her.

As Christine Goodier explains in *1612: The Lancashire Witch Trials*, Catholic rebellions had swarmed northern England in 1537, which ended with the public execution of the last abbot of Lancashire. The "Anglican Church [failed] to fill the void left by the destruction of the abbey, leaving people, if the testimony given in 1612 is to be believed, to rely on their memories of old Catholic rites and teachings to fill their lives with meaning." To Catholics in continental Europe, demons and witches were anathema to their beliefs, but to Anglicans, the link between Catholicism and witchcraft was clear as day.

Following secret Catholic rites to another Lancashire hot spot, I left the tour to hole up at Samlesbury Hall. In 1612, Samlesbury Hall was home to another witchcraft scandal that ran concurrently with the one in Pendle. While I walked its manicured grounds, burnt orange, yellow, and crimson leaves spun from the trees around the black-and-white half-timbered manor. Animals in pens and beekeepers were bustling out back, while a massive carrot cake was being served with tea inside.

Erected in 1325, Samlesbury boasts a great medieval hall with stained glass, ironwork, and a crackling fireplace painted in red, gold, and blue motifs around coats of arms. The witchcraft incident associated with the hall involved a fourteen-year-old girl who was coached by a Catholic priest to accuse three older women of being part of a cannibalistic, child-killing coven straight out of continental demonology.

Samlesbury was a haven for Catholics at the time, and the building still has a hidden alcove in the fireplace where priests would camp out away from the sight of nosy Anglican authorities.

Unlike the Pendle witches, the Samlesbury witches were vindicated and the accusations against them were revealed to be lies. But witchcraft reeking of Catholicism coupled with cunning practices would lead to the deaths of Demdike (who died in jail) as well as Elizabeth Device, Alizon Device, James Device, Chattox, Anne Redfearne, and multiple others whom Jennet Device fingered for being at the Malkin Tower meal. (This includes Alice Nutter, who was not a cunning woman nor had cause to consort with such people as the Devices and is now commemorated by a statue near the place she once lived in Roughlee.)

My final hours in Lancashire were spent where the Pendle witches spent theirs: at Lancaster Castle. Nearly a thousand years of history have played out on the spot where the imposing stone castle now perches above the city. It was in the dank, sunless dungeon here that the octogenarian Demdike died, and the rest of the accused witches were held until their hanging. Tourists aren't allowed into its depths now, but the entrance to the dungeon is still visible through a rusted gate. You can, however, tour the very courtroom where the Pendle witches argued their last, and where Jennet Device sealed the fates of her family, egged on by an eager Roger Nowell.

It is clear that acts of folk magic mingled with interpersonal conflict in Pendle, and that many innocents were ensnared in the pandemonium. But what was the real relationship between the Device family and their animal familiars? Were these cunning folk *actually* cursing and killing their neighbors? All we know for certain is how the trials ended. On Thursday, August 20, 1612, the accused witches were all hanged a short distance from Lancaster Castle. They were given no mercy, no burial, and no grave, to be mourned only by their kin and—as Duffy's bleak memorial poem puts it—"future tourists who might grieve."

THE PASSION OF KING JAMES

Edinburgh, Scotland

THE COLLAR LOOKED JUST LIKE one of mine. The kind I've worn to club nights and office jobs—the kind I clung to in my teenage years to telegraph my toughness when I was trying not to be a trembling leaf of a girl. I saw it from across the room, and a flood of memories propelled me toward the relic enshrined in glass. A thick band fitted with an o-ring stretched from throat to chest. Small triangular points ringed the top and bottom rims. With a formidable width and heft, it would no doubt command an eye-catching, elegant posture in its wearer: chin up, back straight, vertebrae coaxed into alignment. It was a statement piece, to say the least.

Unlike one of my mine, though, it wasn't leather, but iron. Rusted from years of disuse, the collar was the color of graveyard dirt: chthonic dark chocolate. Its sharp edges weren't for fashionable or pleasurable play, and it was not for suiting up to go out at night—well, not by choice. The girl or woman who would have found herself in it was not being coquettish while she wore it. There was no sparkle in her eye, no smile lying in wait behind her perfectly posed snarl. She had no say in how it even got around her neck, the metal teeth locking in place, forced by a rough hand with no interest in seeing her survive to see it removed.

This "Witch's collar," as the label in the National Museum of Scotland noted grimly, was not some daring accoutrement like the ones in my closet, but a carceral relic of the Scottish witch hunts. Suspended on a pedestal, it was the most relatable piece in the section on sorcery in the museum's stark white rooms. Cursing my eyesight, I chided myself for coveting it from afar. The collar—from Ladybank, a town in the nearby borough of Fife—told a gruesome story of state-sponsored violence.

"I think this is really cruel," reads the text next to the collar, attributed to a young—and rightfully agitated—member of the museum's Junior Board. "It's a way of trying to get someone (usually a woman) suspected of witchcraft to confess to being a witch. I can just imagine the jagged points making her neck bleed. Sometimes all women did to be suspected was to talk in their sleep or mumble!"

The collar wasn't the only device on display. It was joined by a mighty set of manacles and chains, not one, but two types of thumbscrews, and an iron gag also known as a "witches' bridle." A hinged, iron muzzle featuring a metal headpiece attached to a bridle bit, the witches' bridle would have been inserted into an accused witch's mouth to curb any kind of vocalization. This contraption was also called a "scold's bridle" and was frequently used on outspoken crones or members of the fairer sex prone to gossip. Really, any kind of woman who wielded words in provocative ways. If you didn't hold your tongue, it would be quite literally held for you.

Surveying this tableau, it was painfully evident to me that Scottish witch hunting was a particularly nasty business. But it's not as if the idea of witches suddenly appeared out of nowhere. So when exactly did witches become enemies of Scotland—and why?

WITCH HUNT

"For centuries before about 1550, people had believed in witches; malevolent old women casting evil spells were standard folklore characters," explains Julian Goodare in *The Scottish Witch Hunt in Context*. "However, medieval people do not seem to have been *haunted* by these beliefs, and they had not acted on them; there had been no witch hunt. Now, with the Reformation and the growth of the modern state, there was."

As happened all across Europe, the Scots began to focus on witches as being responsible for the conflicts and clashes endemic to their changing society. These culprits were singled out by the king, the citizenry, the courts, and the Protestant clergy, and 85 percent of them were women.

As Brian P. Levack notes in *Witch-Hunting in Scotland*, "A Scottish woman in the seventeenth century was twelve times more likely than her English counterpart to be executed for witchcraft." She was also likelier to be subject to violence. Scottish and English law both required special warrants for torture, but Scottish authorities were far more lax about enforcing their torture laws.

Turning my attention back to the display case, I saw the supposed ringleader of these Scottish witches reveling in his powers. Above the instruments of torture I had spent so much time looking at, the Devil, with horns erect and claws unsheathed, preached to a coterie of enthralled women. In a 1591 woodcut print from the pamphlet *Newes from Scotland*, the seas tossed a ship. Four demonic folk cooked an unholy concoction in the corner. Something sinister was afoot.

In Edinburgh the weather is fickle. Tempestuous and wet transforms into a momentary scorch. Grass ripples with the warm breeze, then shivers beneath the wind's brisk breath.

Always at risk of experiencing four seasons in a single day, the weather is a constant reminder you're subject to the whims of something—or someone—else.

In 1590, the weather was beset by witches. The seas became a cauldron, roiling and pungent. The stars snuffed out one by one. Royal journeys of the utmost importance had recently been afflicted with mysteriously bad weather, so when waves began to batter the sides of King James VI's ship as he returned to Scotland from Denmark with his new bride, Queen Anne, the only explanation was witchcraft.

Shortly after the couple's harrowing journey, a few treacherous women of Copenhagen confessed to thwarting an earlier voyage that Queen Anne endured. (It was a commonly held belief in Scandinavia that witches could brew up storms.) When the accused witches burned in Kronborg because of their malicious magic, James's fears did not die with them. Plague-like, fear began to fester across the North Sea, infecting the people of Edinburgh.

The king was obsessed with the idea of the Devil disrupting his rule. He began to believe that another coven might also be to blame for the weather delays he and his wife encountered—that it wasn't only Danish witches who wished him and Queen Anne ill, but Scottish ones as well. He heard they had danced in the dark on the sands of North Berwick— twenty miles northeast of Edinburgh as the crow flies—and the Devil had joined them in a ritual designed to sabotage his sovereignty.

The remnants of Saint Andrew's Old Kirk where these witches manifested their misdeeds into action are still there, but barely. What remains at the former site of medieval pilgrimage from the twelfth century are a few crumbling stone walls. The rest was swallowed by a hungry sea years ago.

Now, there are restaurants, shops, and amusements sprinkled across the waterfront. (The puffins at the Scottish Seabird Centre are a particularly adorable sight.) But in the late sixteenth century, this chilling promontory was where Geillis Duncan and Agnes Sampson confessed they and other witches had joined in a Satanic sabbath.

Geillis, also known as Gelie Duncan, was the teenage maidservant of bailie David Seton. She was supposedly capable of "many matters most miraculous," according to *Newes from Scotland*, and her healing abilities were suspect, begotten from "extraordinary and unlawful means." In a move that Seton likely believed would earn accolades from the king, he and his son began to torture Duncan. After they shaved her body to search for the Devil's mark, applied thumbscrews to pierce through the flesh of her nail beds, and subjected her body to other excruciating tortures, she succumbed and confessed. Duncan confirmed she was a witch, and that she had other accomplices, too, including a schoolmaster, two wealthy Edinburgh socialites, and Agnes Sampson, a local midwife.

King James soon got involved. There had been other recent threats to his rule, and he wasted no time. Kings were not usually wont to partake so intimately in such affairs. In fact, there is no parallel occurrence in any other country during the early modern witch hunts. But James was not your usual monarch when it came to witches.

The king decreed that Agnes Sampson should be brought into Holyroodhouse and examined. She was not the only suspect he interrogated, but their exchange is the most famed. At first, Agnes denied any involvement when questioned about cursing James's travels. But that was before she was chained up in a cell, fastened to a wall with a witches' bridle thrust into her mouth. She was denied sleep, and a rope was tied around her neck. After hours of unimaginable torture, her head was shaved and her body searched for any telltale signs of deviance.

Then, as *Newes from Scotland* would credulously report, examiners discovered some sort of mark on Agnes's genital area, and she confessed at once. She told tales of eleven different witch meetings, including one in North Berwick. Sampson described the details of a black mass where she and other witches danced and drank. She spoke of the healing and midwifery which she had practiced for years. She told of how she had helped tie human parts onto the body of a dead cat, then heaved it into the sea in Leith to conjure a storm to kill James.

Despite this overflow of damning information, the king did not believe her. So Agnes invited the king to listen carefully. She revealed knowledge of the words he and his wife had shared on the night of their wedding. They were supposedly exact. And so James's skepticism was allayed. He believed Sampson had sight beyond sight. She was sentenced to death, then strangled, and her body burned next to the castle just as Geillis Duncan had been and hundreds of others would be in the coming century.

Just outside the castle where King James once tore about, possessed by his monomania for witches, is a stately stone building where I was happily entombed. Inside the Old Rectory, I was giddy on champagne and the prospect of perverting an ecclesiastical suite with my presence. It was as if a bishop had just left his quarters for an evening constitutional, and as the sun slipped below the horizon, I slipped inside and dead bolted the door, unpacking a suitcase filled with his worst nightmares: a glamour magic ritual oil handcrafted by witches, tarot cards depicting intimate queer couplings, a "She Devil" ring carved out of silver, and leather heels cut with inverted crosses. I was suddenly back in Episcopal school or supping with the very Catholic side of my family and wanted nothing more than to *make a scene*. Seeing as no one was around to enjoy my childish protest, I settled for a few sacrilegious selfies instead.

Constructed for merchant Thomas Lowthian in 1595, the home is also a stone's throw from Castlehill, where hundreds of accused witches met their fiery deaths. This hearty residence would become part of the landscape of Edinburgh during the terror-filled years when diablerie consumed the mind of the monarch: shortly after Lowthian moved in, King James wrote and published his malicious magnum opus, *Daemon-ologie*, which further fueled the fires of Castlehill and a belief in Satanic witchcraft in the British Isles.

Now a restaurant and hotel known, ironically, as The Witchery, Lowthian's former abode still has touches of the original design, including his initials and his maxim, "O Lord in thee is all my traist," chiseled into the aging stone above the entrance. One noticeable addition is a wooden sign with a serpent slithering around a pitchfork, a flaming torch, an inverted tree, and a horned devil's face, among other ominous things. The lights on the outside of the building are crimson, tipped toward the roof. At night, they cast bloody streaks up the walls and into the sky, a visual reminder of how much blood has been spilled so near this spot.

The Witchery offers only a few select rooms in which you can stay the night. (Actress Dannii Minogue called it "the perfect lust den.") Branching off a winding stone turnpike staircase, these rooms are named after their eclectic decor—Armoury, Vestry, Sempill—all of which veer between delightfully campy and period-themed elegant.

Everything in my room, the Old Rectory, was plucked from the past. Red and gold and deeply devout, it was heavy with old money opulence: Gothic with a capital G. A knight's full suit of armor stood at attention in the corner. Leather-bound books reclined on shelves that opened up to become secret closets. The latter few Commandments were emblazoned on the wall, a reminder that so few of us can truly pass Christian muster. (I confess, I coveted the entire place.)

After a delicious, candlelit dinner in The Witchery's restaurant where I was the only person dining alone without a lover to sidle up to, I returned to the Old Rectory for a soak. Red and gold lion wallpaper covered the bathroom. A man in a red uniform watched me sternly from his place immortalized in a portrait near the luxurious tub. I floated contently in water that had been charged with the glamour oil I had brought from home and a hibiscus seed oil I had bought from San Miniato in Florence. The former was made by a hoodoo priestess; the latter, a monk. My bathwater will be syncretic, if nothing else.

The oak bed fashioned from antique pulpits was the centerpiece of the room. Lying back under the duvet at night, skyclad, I imagined what kind of life I could have had in the sixteenth or seventeenth century. Plenty of my personal attributes could make me a target of the hunts. The poorest along with the wealthy, learned, and powerful were swept up in their current, so why *not* me? It could easily have been my screams coming from the outside, muffled by the thick stone walls; my body burning on Castlehill, not shrouded in red velvet and gold tassles, a fully stocked tray of tea and cookies and white linen napkins bound in red ribbons by my bedside.

I tried to mediate between my conflicting thoughts about being inside this very opulent yet agitating building. I sat up with eyes closed, offering a stream of consciousness incantation to honor those who never got a chance. I fumbled to find the right words to commemorate the unimaginable deaths of strangers whose suffering has brought such appeal to a place where tourists can now indulge their appetites for the macabre and a meal. The thrill of the place fizzled at the thought. My joy stuck in my throat.

I had a fitful night's sleep, but woke ready to make the most of my final hours in The Witchery. After years of research, I was well versed in the internal conflict, debate, and ambivalence that the venture of witch tourism consistently inspires.

Later that morning, I tried to pay my respects at the modest Witches' Well—a few paces from the hotel—which memorializes those executed for witchcraft in Edinburgh. But the monarchy had other plans, so instead I sat trapped in The Witchery's restaurant glutting myself on a full English breakfast as my waiter and I peered out the window of the subterranean space just in time to see the Honours of Scotland.

Driving by in an old-fashioned coach with oversize glass windows, the red and gold fur-adorned crown was the same one that sat on the head of King James, and it was moving down the Royal Mile toward a special session of Parliament where the queen was waiting. A large bust of the Devil grinned back at me next to the window, and the way the waiter and I craned our necks to see the processional was not unlike what those had done centuries before during an execution—a fact the waiter noted only after the crown had passed. Lowthian's home would have given you a near front-row seat to the condemned, whose bodies, post-strangulation, were set aflame as crowds cheered and jeered.

When the coast was finally clear, I walked over to the well. Despite the dozens of tourists surrounding the area, I seemed to be the only one interested in this corner of the Royal Mile, right at the entrance to the castle. I took a few pictures before stopping to read the memorial text. Trapped in a bronze relief, a snake slithers up between two women's (two witches') heads and a sprig of foxglove. A healthy bunch of greens that hadn't yet flowered sprouted up where water once flowed. Originally commissioned in 1894 by philanthropist Sir Patrick Geddes, artist John Duncan crafted the memorial for the west side of Castlehill Reservoir drawing from both myth and witch hunting history. The plaque above reads:

> This fountain, designed by John Duncan, R.S.A., is near the site
> on which many witches were burned at the stake. The wicked
> head and serene head signify that some used their exceptional
> knowledge for evil purposes while others were misunderstood
> and wished their kind nothing but good. The serpent has the
> dual significance of evil and wisdom. The Foxglove spray further
> emphasises the dual purpose of many common objects.

I was taken aback by the stance that the memorial makers took on witches and witchcraft. To them, the women and men who died here were *all* spellcasters—only some were evil and some good. This was not political persecution, but merely the old-fashioned binary of black magic versus white magic—with a bit of being caught at the wrong place and the wrong time.

As I took it all in, visitors strolled by, likely oblivious of the witch hunting history surrounding them. I backed away from the well and headed down Castlehill to explore more of Edinburgh. That day, I mentioned my visit to the Witches' Well to multiple friendly locals who inquired what I was up to. All of them had lived in the city their entire lives but had no idea the memorial existed.

After Agnes Sampson, Geillis Duncan, and their "associates" paid the price for their confessed crimes, James's appetite for witch hunting had not been satisfied. Convinced that he remained the greatest enemy of the Devil—as another accused witch had confessed—the king put quill to paper and crafted his treatise *Daemonologie* in 1597. Drawing from continental texts like the *Malleus Maleficarum*, the text was short and not nearly as lurid as those of his predecessors.

"The prurient reader expecting to find salacious details of naked dancing, promiscuous sex between demons and witches, child sacrifice, or cannibalism would be sorely disappointed," Levack writes. "His main concern in describing the sabbath was the way witches aped and mocked Christian services ... [and] whether James's treatise inspired or reflected Scottish witch beliefs, the witches' sabbath in Scotland was a very tame affair indeed."

Thanks to James and his book, witch hunts continued in Scotland aided by the monarch's words. They resulted in the deaths of 1,000 to 2,000 people, yet also served as a method of state-building, unifying Scotland in new ways. Stuart Clark affirms that witch hunting was "at the heart of the reforming process" in "Protestant Demonology." As Scotland was striving for religious renewal and rejecting its Catholic past, witch hunts were one method of spiritual housecleaning.

"The protestant reinvention of a world in which there could only be the forces of good and evil, while undoubtedly well-intended, effectively shattered the grey area once inhabited by witches, charmers and a host of magical beings, consigning them all to the ranks of the Devil, whose power appeared to be growing stronger than ever," explains Lizanne Henderson in "Detestable Slaves of the Devil: Changing Ideas about Witchcraft in Sixteenth-Century Scotland." In King James's country, you were either with him or against him.

By 1603, James VI of Scotland was crowned king of England, unifying Scotland, England, and Ireland into a single Protestant empire as he become James I. A year later, James masterminded the 1604 Witchcraft Act for the entire kingdom, which escalated punishments for those convicted of witchcraft. As the king's power grew, he decided to commission a new version of the Bible to replace all previous and "inaccurate" versions. His dedication to Protestant piety and the witch hunting waves he set in motion would have a lasting impact on his own country—and a few fledgling colonies across the Atlantic. By 1606, Shakespeare's *Macbeth* was being performed across England, featuring three tempest-raising witches who cause quite a stir in a Scottish king's empire. When it comes to witches, the truth is always far stranger than fiction.

WITCHES OF AMERICA
Williamsburg and Jamestown, Virginia

THE WOODS ARE DENSE AND VERDANT around Jamestown. Deer leap between dark clusters of trees where the ground isn't thick with swamp or marsh. Osprey hover above the James River, stalking fish. Save for a single parkway cutting through, the land is mostly untouched, offering a glimpse of what the English saw when they first settled on the isthmus in 1607.

During the first few years of the seventeenth century, James I had become the ruler of a vastly expanded kingdom, but his country's economy was in decline. In a bid to spread Anglican doctrine, tap into the natural resources of Virginia, and compete with the Spanish who were gaining a foothold in the "New World," the king approved a charter to start the Virginia colony in 1606. It would be the first of thirteen that would later coalesce into the United States.

I drove from Richmond to Jamestown late at night, no lights on the highway but high beams and the glowing eyes of animals in the trees. My destination was the Historic Powhatan Resort, named after the indigenous tribe that inhabited the region for centuries before the English brought guns, disease, and witchcraft. Jamestown colonizer Captain John Smith had nothing but noxious words when meeting Chief Powhatan, describing him as "more like a devil than a man."

I came to Virginia in search of the early modern American Devil and his faithful servant, the witch. Little did I know that turning the TV on in my room at the resort, I would be treated to Protestant preaching straight out of the colonial past. Settling in for bed, I alighted on *The 700 Club*, evangelical minister Pat Robertson's long-running show on air since 1966. I watched Robertson tell a man his gay son was in the Devil's clutches. He then spoke of the subservient role God wants women to take in their relationships with men. I listened to Robertson try to heal the sick with impassioned prayer. One viewer appeared on camera to say her chronic migraines had been cured by the nonagenarian. "The Devil didn't win this time," she announced, joyously. "I did."

This is the same Pat Robertson who once spoke out in vehement opposition against the Equal Rights Amendment in 1992, writing an open letter to the Christian Coalition expressing his distaste for gender equality. The "feminist agenda," he wrote, "is about a socialist, anti-family political movement that encourages women to leave their husbands, kill their children, practice witchcraft, destroy capitalism and become lesbians." (In a way, he wasn't *all* wrong . . .)

Many of the early Protestant beliefs foundational to Robertson's evangelism—and the modern evangelical movement—came directly from England to the colonies when witch hunts still raged. In fact, some scholars have deemed Puritan minister Cotton Mather—famed for his role in the Salem trials—"the first American evangelical."

When I could stomach *The 700 Club* no more, I turned the TV off. Gazing out at the bucolic grounds outside my room, I fell asleep pondering just how much and how little the American religious landscape has changed since the days of King James.

The next morning, I set out early to visit the Jamestown Settlement. Inside the visitor center, a temporary exhibition called "Tenacity" was on view, exploring the lives of real women who once lived in Jamestown: Powhatan, English, and West African. A variety of artifacts populated the displays, from an embroidered Elizabethan bodice to a ducking stool used to punish women deemed gossips or scolds. These items revealed a partial picture of life in the seventeenth century, but the accompanying panels offered more insight into women's responsibilities, relationships, and struggles.

Even for the wealthy and white, Jamestown was relatively inhospitable. The early colony was riddled with disease: typhoid, dysentery, scurvy, and salt poisoning ran rampant. Swampland was pervasive, so clean drinking water was hard to come by, and food shortages even led the fledgling colony to cannibalism within the first few years of its founding. Amid such life-threatening hardships, the colonists first and foremost looked to indigenous people as a source of evil. The foreign Powhatan religion was viewed as unsettling and bizarre—and reeked of witchcraft to English eyes. "Their priests," wrote Reverend Alexander Whitaker in 1612, "are no other but such as our English witches are. They live naked in bodie, as if their shame of their sinne deserved no covering."

Alison Games explains in *Witchcraft in Early North America* that those "launching evangelical missions in North America were optimistic that the Devil could be displaced." In 1613, William Crashaw affirmed the duty to continue to colonize—and Christianize—the land, concurring with Whitaker's view of Virginia. "Satan visibly and palpably raignes there," he wrote, "more than any other known place of the world: yet be of courage . . . God will treade Satan under your feet shortly."

There are no records of the English trying any Indians in court for the crime of witchcraft. It would take another decade until the colonists began to look within their ranks for unholy crimes.

"Beginning in the mid-1620s, as the Virginia colony grew with new arrivals, the English settlers began to find disciples of the devil in their own communities," writes Carson O. Hudson in *Witchcraft in Colonial Virginia*. "From then until the early eighteenth century, the colony's surviving records indicate several witchcraft investigations, petitions, slander suits and countersuits."

Joan Wright is the first known woman accused of witchcraft in America. She arrived at Jamestown in 1609 from Hull, a port town in the northeast of England. Within a year, she had married her husband Robert, who himself would run in and out of trouble with the law as a notorious debtor. Earlier in life, Wright was whipped for not sewing a shirt correctly. Years later, she was a midwife a bit too good at knowing when those in her community weren't well—and when husbands or hens were about to die. She was also left-handed, a feature that marked her as odd, if not nefarious. Colonial Virginians eventually had enough of her ill-omened speech, and she was branded a witch.

A short drive from the Jamestown Settlement is Historic Jamestowne, the heart of the first colony. There, on a gently sloping stretch of land dotted with oak trees, sunlight dapples the James River as it laps at the shore. Some of what used to stand in the old fort has been partially reconstructed based on the work of archaeologists. Visitors walking through the site—which remains in various states of excavation—can see where the well, the storehouse, the barracks, and the first church once stood, where Powhatan Pocahontas (given name Matoaka) married Englishman and tobacco farmer John Rolfe. The most fascinating items dug up at Jamestown are housed on-site at the Voorhees Archaearium archaeology museum. Under glass portals in its floors, you can view the original foundations of the Jamestown General Court where Joan Wright stood trial in September of 1626.

Over a dozen people spoke out against Goodwife Wright. According to one testimony, Wright was supposed to deliver a child, but the mother changed her mind after learning Wright was left-handed and requested another midwife. Wright took her leave of the family's house "very much discontented," and shortly thereafter, the mother, father, and child fell ill in succession. The child eventually died. In a similar case, Wright was passed over yet again to assist with a birth, and the newborn delivered by another midwife passed away. More testimony swore that Wright had been a witch back in England and retained knowledge of how to combat witchcraft—as any good cunning woman would. All you had to do was heat a horseshoe in the fires of an oven until it was "red hott," and then fling it into urine to make a witch "sick at the harte." (Throughout colonial Virginia, an upside-down horseshoe nailed over a door or hearth was used to ward off witches, but witch bottles were common, too.) Wright's trial records indicate that she wasn't all that bothered about being called a witch by her neighbors, though. She reportedly "made light of it," saying, "God forgive them."

"The accusations against Wright and her response before the Virginia Council illustrate one of the important features of English beliefs," Alison Games notes, "the relative insignificance of the Devil and the Devil's pact. Both elements would emerge as characteristics in outbreaks, but for the most part witchcraft accusations in English colonies centered not on diabolism but rather on maleficia."

We know that Wright was tried in the Jamestown court, but the verdict and what happened to her afterward were destroyed during the Civil War. It is quite unlikely Wright was killed, however. The only known woman executed for witchcraft near the colony was Kathryn Grady, the victim of vigilante "justice" aboard a ship destined for Virginia that ran into rough waters in 1654, for which she was blamed.

Recently, the Jamestown Settlement mounted a play, *Season of the Witch*, based on Joan Wright's trial transcripts. Every October, both the Settlement and Historic Jamestowne feature some sort of witchcraft-related event for the Halloween season, shining a light once more on the colony's women once deemed witches.

Time stands still in Colonial Williamsburg. The world's largest living history museum has been built to thrive as the city once did before the Revolutionary War. Gallivant down the mile-long Duke of Gloucester Street, and you can tip the wrist at historic taverns, watch horse-drawn carriages careen by, and explore the Blacksmith's, the Joiner's, the Printer's, the Milliner's, and the Wig Maker's. Inside these quaint buildings are people—not actors—trained in their trades, busy crafting goods just as they would have in the eighteenth century.

At the Silversmith's, I was privy to delicate tablewares in the midst of fabrication. A single silver bowl can take days to produce in the traditional way, the master silversmith said. At the Printer's, I watched a tradesman gathering single metal pieces each stamped with a different letter to create a holiday greeting. This painstaking work was how early modern witchcraft pamphlets were made. At the Apothecary's, the shelves are stacked with jars and bottles filled with herbs and powders that colonial people would have wandered inside to buy. A woman working in a cap and dress was answering questions from guests, so I inquired about the historical difference between midwives and doctors. She explained that pregnancy was not viewed as an ailment back then, and thus not the province of doctors—unless there were complications, of course.

Colonial Williamsburg isn't entirely accessible by car, so a bus cycles through various stops around the perimeter to take you from one area to the next. Each time I climbed aboard, a recorded greeting reminded me to curb my speech. "Please abstain from inappropriate or disrespectful language," a woman's voice announced through the bus speakers, invoking a bygone time when women's words were frequently criminalized.

In 1662, the Virginia House of Burgesses passed a law about disorderly female speech that stated "brabling" women would be punished by ducking—the same punishment King James suggests for witches in *Daemonologie*.

As Terri L. Snyder notes in *Brabbling Women: Disorderly Speech and the Law in Early Virginia*, "*brabbling* signified a wrangling, quibbling, quarrelsome, or riotous disposition. It was not an expressly gendered term, but Virginia's lawmakers chose to inflect it as such in the text of the law and the punishment it described." Joan Wright was clearly a "brabling" woman, and in New England witchcraft cases, disorderly speech was often used as evidence that a woman was a witch.

Down the main thoroughfare past the trade shops, I came upon a garden growing traditional colonial plants like Scotch kale, leeks, poppies, sorrel, scurvy grass, purple turnip, and prickly pear. Turnip and mint were commonly used to battle coughs and stomachaches, the women tending to the neat rows of flowers and greens told me.

Across the street, the fife-and-drum corps played the sun below the horizon. Marching in formation with red coats and cream-colored breeches, the corps executed Scottish and English traditional songs with precision. Nearby, I spied a working couple in colonial garb: her skirts billowing, his tricorn pointed due north as they walked arm in arm down the cobblestone street past tourists pretending to be stuck in the stocks. A nearby sign encouraged us to tag such pictures with the hashtag #colonialmugshots.

Cannons fired at dusk, and students from the College of William and Mary next door ran down Duke of Gloucester Street or walked their dogs among the tourists. I wandered into an off-site coffee shop and sipped tea next to a woman in colonial costume. She gripped her cup of coffee in one hand as she hid the unruly wisps of hair that escaped her white cap with the other. Once it was fully dark, I ventured back inside Colonial Williamsburg to a candlelit courtroom for a witch trial.

Joan Wright may have been the first witch of Virginia, but the colony's last would be far more famous. Grace Sherwood, known today as the "Witch of Pungo" or, more simply, the "Virginia Witch," was in and out of courtrooms for years because of her malevolent reputation.

In 1697, Grace and her husband James sued a man for defamation after he called her a witch. They requested the sum of fifty pounds sterling, but the case was settled out of court. Sherwood would sue for defamation again in 1698, when a different man and his wife said Grace had "bewitched their pigs to death and bewitched their cotton." Concurrently, another woman professed that Grace came to her at night and "rid her and went out the key hole or crack of the door like a black catt." In turn, Grace and her husband sued both parties for slander, asking one hundred pounds sterling, each. The jury denied the Sherwoods' claim, and Grace was left with her bad name intact.

In 1705, four years after her husband left her widowed, Grace got into a physical altercation with a neighbor who had called her a witch, and she brought the complaint to court. The jury found in Grace's favor, awarding her one pound in damages. Angered by their loss, the neighbor and her husband brought a formal charge of witchcraft against Grace in 1706. Following witch protocol set in England, a jury of women was brought in to search Grace Sherwood's body for any suspicious marks. (Unfortunately for Grace, a woman she had previously sued for slander served as forewoman of said group.) Upon examining Sherwood, the women announced that they had found "two things like titts with severall other spotts." Grace was taken into custody and eventually put to a water test. She was bound by rope around her hands and feet and thrown in the water. Those present observed Grace carefully to see if she would float or sink to determine if she was a witch. Unfortunately, Grace floated, "contrary to custom."

Sherwood's story is so memorable that a statue of her stands today in Virginia Beach, and she is the star of a weekly play performed at Colonial Williamsburg. Some even suggest that Grace Sherwood herself haunts the productions.

Cry Witch, written and directed by historian Carson O. Hudson, is drawn from the records of Grace Sherwood's 1706 trial for witchcraft. The line queued up outside the historic Capitol building for the play—the same grounds where the original trial took place—was packed with chattering teenage students on a field trip. Once we had filed in and were seated, the gentleman jurors entered and took their places in the jury box. "Abandon your twenty-first century mindsets" declared the bewigged man introducing the play, and *Cry Witch* began with the accusations against Sherwood read aloud, followed by live witness testimonies.

Cry Witch is designed to incorporate audience interaction, and so the students obliged, addressing their queries about the evidence presented to the governor who presided over the trial. Some witnesses were more measured than others. One woman was in a deeply agitated state as she attested that Grace came into her home at night to afflict her with witchcraft. The audience was then asked to vote on Sherwood's guilt or innocence, and based on so many negative accusations, the group overwhelmingly leaned toward guilty. Sherwood would soon dissolve into her own agitated state, falling into a fit of hopeless screaming when the verdict was announced.

My foray into the American witch trials felt like a continuation of the English trials in certain respects. However, in Virginia, accusations were all small-scale, at the individual level. But what makes studying the Virginia witch hunts of the seventeenth and eighteenth centuries particularly disturbing is the historical backdrop against which they took place. Walking the streets of Colonial Williamsburg, I saw actors playing Indians and Africans living in various states of subjugation as they would have among the European colonists, an important reminder that white women accused of witchcraft were hardly experiencing persecution on the scale that indigenous and enslaved people living around them were.

America was built on stolen indigenous territory and flourished because of slave labor. Because of that fact, it can feel foolish to dwell on witch persecutions—on gender-based oppression—alone. And yet, examining the witch trials in colonial America is crucial to understanding American history and to grasping how Europeans settlers and their descendants would eventually come to define themselves as "white" in opposition to a racialized "other." This process was, in fact, tied to aspects of witch hunting.

In *Good Wives, Nasty Wenches & Anxious Patriarchs: Gender, Race, and Power in Colonial Virginia*, Kathleen M. Brown describes how gender became increasingly "scrutinized by the court and church alike" in late sixteenth-century England, becoming "an important technology of state power—both at home and abroad." This is her explanation for the rise in witchcraft cases at the time. "Parliament's decision to criminalize witchcraft," Brown explains, "tightened the connections between gender ideologies and state power by reiterating categories of deviance and encouraging community efforts to enforce conformity."

Accusations of witchcraft were one way to police women who strayed from behaving in accordance with patriarchal standards. Or, as Christina Larner puts it in *Enemies of God*: "The women who were accused were those who challenged the patriarchal view of the ideal woman." However, the move to legislate the hierarchy of gender would also go on to impact conceptions of racial hierarchies as well. "Discourses of gender, the division of labor by sex, and the regulation of white women's sexuality were integral to the process of defining race and contributed significantly to the establishment of slavery in Virginia during the seventeenth century," Brown argues.

Even when examining the persecution of white women by the church, state, and their own communities, the specter of racism and colonialism hovers nearby, adding a new dimension to witch accusations that did not exist in Europe. The interplay between race, sex, and gender-based oppression has birthed a thorny, complex legacy that endures in contemporary US politics and culture. When delving into the American witch trials, it cannot be ignored.

The morning after I saw *Cry Witch*, I visited Grace Sherwood in a hospital parking lot. A beautiful bronze memorial to Virginia's famed, final sorceress is accompanied by a plaque with the words of then-governor Tim Kaine, who exonerated Grace posthumously in 2006. What happened to Grace after she was declared a witch at her ducking is unknown, but there is evidence that she received a grant for land in 1714, so she was likely jailed and then released. Her last will and testament were probated in 1740 by her sons, making Grace around eighty when she died.

The Grace Sherwood statue is near a highway, a hospital, and a Walgreens. It is a very forgettable place for a memorial, and no one was parked anywhere near me when I arrived. However, there were traces of recent visitors. In Grace's hand is a bronze basket of herbs, but someone had placed a bouquet of live roses there that had barely begun to wilt. At her feet, a raccoon stands on its hind legs, a paw tugging on Grace's skirts. Local lore embellished Sherwood's legacy to include the skills of midwifery and the ability to communicate with animals and to heal with herbs. How much of that is true, we'll never know. What we do know is that she was ducked where Witchduck Road now dead-ends at the water. Old Donation Church down the street features a gravestone-shaped memorial to Grace in a small garden. And every year at the Pungo Strawberry Festival, an honorary "Witch of Pungo" is named.

The surrounding area of Virginia Beach has a surprisingly large concentration of metaphysical, New Age, and witch shops. I visited a few, cognizant of how much has changed for witchcraft to be normalized—as it has in London, Paris, Florence, and beyond. But it is not as if witchcraft has been completely accepted, either. Today, the contemporary evangelical community retains great political power in this country, and many of its members do indeed still believe in the Devil—and Satanic witches, too. Though Protestantism and the belief in witchcraft may have come from Europe, it manifested in America in uniquely American ways.

MARITIME MALEFICIA
Rehoboth Beach, Delaware

THE CHESAPEAKE BAY RAGED a hundred feet below. Whitecaps hurled themselves onto wooden pilings, while sailboats dipped horizontal before righting themselves again. I sped across the Bay Bridge, rain pelting my windshield, eyes darting down to the turbulent waters I had traversed so many times before. Even in the storm, this scenic crossing was a comfort, but the accused witches aboard ships once destined for the Chesapeake did not survive to see its beauty. Born and raised in close proximity to the bay, I wasn't privy to tales of Mid-Atlantic *maleficia* until adulthood. But women accused of witchcraft did live and die here, their stories drowned out by Salem or the hungry waters that swallowed them up centuries ago.

In 1654, a passenger ship called the *Charity* set sail from London destined for Saint Mary's City. By all accounts, the voyage was cursed from the start. Within days of the ship leaving port, the Atlantic Ocean began to swell, and the skies blackened. Onyx whirlpools spun the *Charity* dizzy. Waves crested, then crashed onto the deck as leaks sprang in the ship both fore and aft. Saltwater seared the skin of all who ventured up from the hold below. As the crew broke their backs trying to salvage the vessel, superstition spread. This was no simple squall, the seamen declared to one another in ragged whispers, as if speaking their fears aloud would only cause further calamity. After weeks of bailing water and fighting to keep their rations dry and their ship afloat, the whispers turned to shouts. Panic slithered up the captain's spine when he caught wind of what his men believed.

Belowdecks, Mary Lee knew nothing but the ocean's acrimony. An older widow traveling alone, rumor and hearsay had clung to her since the moment she came aboard. Day after day, the ship rocked Mary into a nauseated daze as she huddled in the corner, waiting out the stormy passage. The floor was slick with water and sick. Mary clung to whatever she could for balance with the rest of the beleaguered passengers, sucking down crusts of moldy bread for sustenance. The wind shrieked banshee-like, a harbinger of her coming fate.

For over two months—most of the voyage from London to Maryland—the ocean's undulations were paired with constant prayer. There was no sign of respite from rain pouring and waves pummeling the ship, so the seamen knew what had to be done whether the captain gave it his blessing or not. Charging into the hold screaming of witchcraft one night, two crew members grabbed Mary. Seething with adrenaline and righteous anger, they shook her to her feet. Mary had summoned the maelstrom. She was a witch, they believed, and she was to blame for the ship's misfortune.

The seamen dragged Mary's frail body out into the storm. Soaked to the bone, Mary's petticoat dragged behind her, becoming the only resistance she could muster against her accusers. They ripped open her bodice and began to search her for the mark of a witch. Twisting her flesh this way and that, they found something on her skin to satisfy their suppositions, so Mary was carried to the capstan and lashed there for the night to prolong her punishment.

The next morning, Mary was weak and fading. Left out in the elements for hours, she was delirious and confessed to all that she had been accused of: to crafting storms; to cursing ships. The captain resisted the news at first, then caved to his crew's allegations. At the sailors' insistence, Mary Lee was hanged and her body tossed into the ocean along with her meager belongings. The Atlantic became a roiling River Styx, ushering Mary from this world to the next. But the storm still did not let up.

When the *Charity* finally docked in Saint Mary's City, the local colonial government began an investigation into Mary's murder. Multiple recorded statements confirm her treatment and the black magic beliefs of the men working on the ship, but no one was charged with Mary Lee's violent death.

A few years later in 1658, Elizabeth Richardson and Katherine Grady would fall victim to similar fates on two different ships also bound for the Chesapeake. Bad weather and bad witches were thought to go hand in hand, and vigilante justice prevailed in all three cases despite documented objections from others on board.

"Court records characterized all three of the Chesapeake travelers as old," Alison Games writes. "Possibly there was something about these women's behavior—either physical manifestations, maladies, odd spasms, muttered prayers, superstitious acts, or unpleasant dispositions—that marked them as witches." Whatever it was that aroused suspicions, Lee, Richardson, and Grady were not even given the luxury of an (un)fair trial. "Certainly their rapid identification by their fellow travelers points to the tenacity of the English expectations about witches," Games continues, "that they were likely to be elderly women and that they could be a particular menace at sea."

My morning drive continued from Maryland to Delaware and down the Delmarva Peninsula as the rain began to lift. Sunlight pierced through thick sylvan enclaves between mobile home parks and clusters of aging brick colonials. Cornfields lay fallow and poultry farms populated the flat landscape between rural towns with only a few storefronts and a single stoplight. When I finally pulled into Rehoboth Beach, the gray sky had transformed to radiant blue. Down the main drag and across the boardwalk I was confronted by hundreds of costumed people milling about, lining up behind barricades, waiting for the festivities to begin—the witch was on her way.

The Rehoboth Beach Sea Witch Festival has been a weekend of parades, contests, and seaside entertainment since 1979. It would be meaningful if the celebration paid homage to unfortunate women like Mary Lee, but that is not the case. Instead, the event is a nod to the lore that Mary fell victim to: the belief that witches conjure shipwrecks, as they have since ancient Greek sirens lured sailors to certain death with their songs.

Witches stirring up storms can be found in early modern English, Scottish, and Scandinavian witchcraft lore—and we know "weather witches" were common in German witch lore, too. But mainland mythology is somewhat distinct from the myths spun by those who spent much of their lives in isolation at sea. "The seaman's worldview combined Christian and pre-Christian beliefs, referents, and orientations," explains Marcus Rediker in *Between the Devil and the Deep Blue Sea*. "Seamen used classical mythology, biblical tales, and traditional yarns as they created their lore and their pantheon of meaningful figures." This Pagan pantheon included sea witches, who were female, like the majority of accused witches. (Really, women of any sort were considered to be unlucky at sea.) Given such associations, English seamen on their way to fledgling ports on the Chesapeake were primed to believe they might encounter acts of maritime *maleficia* on their journeys.

The most notorious sea witch in recent memory is linked to the demise of a British ship, the HMS *DeBraak*, which went down in late May of 1798 off Cape Henlopen in the Delaware Bay. The ship was long thought to protect a glittering treasure, even though every single rescue mission to plunder the wreck failed. By the 1930s, a few would-be treasure hunters searching for the *DeBraak* were themselves caught up in squalls purportedly sent by a "bad weather witch" trying to protect her sunken riches. In an attempt to appease her, the sailors were said to have crafted an effigy of the sea witch, offering her libations and prayers. They then burned the effigy and scattered its ashes, but still the *DeBraak* was nowhere to be found and a hurricane thwarted their final attempt at discovery.

The *DeBraak* remained hidden until it was dredged up and brought ashore in 1986. Inside, excavators found little treasure, but a few items nonetheless smacked of apotropaic magic. Within the *DeBraak* were shards of German stoneware jugs sometimes used to make witch bottles in the seventeenth and eighteenth centuries, as well as a plate with a triangular symbol scratched into its base. These items are now on view at the Zwaanendael Museum in Lewes, Delaware.

Packed tight within the festival crowd, I was overtaken by the salty perfume of battered seafood wafting through the air. Piping hot French fries coated in a dusting of Old Bay seasoning were held fast in costumed fists. Children, adults, and dogs dolled up in cute and spooky disguises flanked me on either side. Most visitors drawn to the Sea Witch Festival come to engage in a seasonal scare, but the celebration does bring its own group of practicing witches as well. Delaware is a hotbed of New Age healers, neo-Pagan practitioners, and witchy women—my own mother included. Small covens and solitary witches alike stalk the boardwalk in black capes, pointed hats, pentacle jewelry, and stylized brooms with their tongues firmly in cheek. But the presence of these Pagan devotees is peripheral, covert even. In a way, the Sea Witch

Festival exemplifies just how much the witch has been defanged and divorced from her history in the American consciousness. Outside the incident in Salem, little is widely known about witches and their persecutions on American shores.

At least 350 cases of witchcraft made it to American colonial courts by the end of the early modern period, the majority of them in the Northeast. Marion Gibson points to thirty-eight to forty documented executions of accused witches across the colonies in *Witchcraft Myths in American Culture*. (All convicted witches were hanged, as burning was not a sanctioned punishment.) There is, however, a likely discrepancy between recorded history and historical fact. Many court records were destroyed in the Civil War, and "it is quite possible that the true number [of executions] was higher ... as witchcraft was a subject of great interest to early Americans," Gibson writes. "There are great stories to be told about American witches and their accusers," she adds, "and also some unexpected contradictions lurking behind the stereotypes to which we have all become accustomed."

Rebecca Fowler remains the only known person executed for witchcraft on Maryland soil, although multiple trials did take place there. A widow living in Calvert County, Fowler was hanged in October 1685 in Saint Mary's City for purportedly causing illness in her community and leaving a few people "very much the worse, consumed, pined & lamed." Historic Saint Mary's City now offers a window into early colonial life along with tours that touch on this history.

The Delaware Valley saw a high-profile witch trial in 1683 when two Swedish women, Margaret Mattson and Yeshro Hendrickson, were accused of *maleficia* by Dutch and English members of their community. The trial was brought to the Provincial Court of Pennsylvania and presided over by Pennsylvania founder William Penn himself. Thanks to

Penn's Quaker lenience, the women were each charged with having the *reputation* of being a witch and thus remanded to their husbands after posting a "peace bond" and promising good behavior. During Halloween season, reenactments of the Mattson trial still take place at Pennsbury Manor in Philadelphia.

Even after the early modern era, people would be accused of malign magic in the Mid-Atlantic region—as they would be across the United States—a little-known history that Owen Davies explores in *America Bewitched: The Story of Witchcraft after Salem.* Despite the pervasive notion that the rise of science and Enlightenment values methodically wiped out a belief in witches and witchcraft, that is not demonstrably true. Skepticism of the supernatural no doubt coursed through the Western world, but belief in black magic held fast in England, too, a phenomenon Thomas Waters exposes in *Cursed Britain: A History of Witchcraft and Black Magic in Modern Times.* For better or for worse, fear of the maleficent witch has never truly gone away.

As I watched the parade, the mob swelled around me, pressing my hips into a metal barricade as a galleon covered in cobwebs manned by skeletons and pirates slid by. All manner of unsettling sea creatures materialized amid a spate of marching musicians before the sea witch herself took center stage. (Her name is Sally.) I tracked a black cat balloon bobbing above as a breeze off the ocean mixed with the scent of saltwater taffy and fresh-made fudge. Children screamed in monstrous timbres, chasing the giant floating green-and-black sea witch head in the sky, as parents got high off frozen custard, caramel popcorn, and Thrasher's fries.

Pushing through the throng of people dancing, laughing, and cheering, I felt pressure in my chest at the sight of so much unbridled joy. Turning toward the once-angry Atlantic, I saw the tide had shifted since the earlier storm. The deep-blue water was calm, gliding across the sand in mesmeric waves, leaving a wake of foam in its path. I headed up over the dunes and down to the beach, which was filled with more people decked out in witch drag. A lone figure in a pointy black hat stood looking out at the horizon in silent reverie. Another green-faced crone lunged at passersby on the boardwalk with mock menace.

Caught in a fun house version of history again, I felt the same disjuncture in Delaware at the Sea Witch Festival that I did in the Harz Mountains. Although far fewer died here, the landscape of the American witch hunts is just as multilayered as Germany's. Rooted in land cast as Satanic since colonizers ripped it away from demonized indigenous peoples, the American witchscape is a place of slavery, dehumanization, and othering where history has been written and rewritten, compressing the most marginal voices into a howling din. But now, across the shores of the Atlantic, the oceanic pull of the archetypal witch that once drove men to murder is cause for celebration. Once captured so she could be controlled and eradicated, the witch now sets so many free. It is an unlikely outcome both bitter and sweet.

RITUALS OF REMEMBRANCE
Hartford, Connecticut

IN HARTFORD, WITCHES BROUGHT ME to church. Days before Halloween, I drove up from New York City through a kaleidoscopic crush of turning leaves. Hartford was a ghost town when I arrived for a morning service honoring the victims of Connecticut's witch hunts. The city was in full-on fright mode—houses wrapped in clouds of cobwebs, storefronts decorated with vampire bats and ghoulish jack-o'-lanterns—but inside Center Church, it was the history of witch hunting that occasioned fear.

Towering over Main Street next to the Ancient Burying Ground, Center Church and its congregation date back to the founding of Hartford in 1636. Center Church was also the spiritual home to some of Hartford's accused witches and witch accusers.

Upon arrival, I passed between the church's imposing Ionic columns and followed the blood-red carpet down the aisle into a well-worn pew. Aside from a few family weddings and funerals, my church attendance over the last twenty years has been quite limited, but I'm game for anything in the name of witches.

The service began with a lecture about New England witch hunting. Dr. Richard S. Ross III spoke about the origins of the diabolical witch, continental demonology, and the English impact on the early modern American witch hunts. Behind him, Jesus hung from the cross in a stained-glass window. The wind tossed the leaves outside on a bright fall day.

Ross cannily laid out the history of witch hunting, eventually speaking of the English Civil War and its impact on American mindsets. When fighting escalated in the 1640s, witch hunting saw a bloody peak in the east of England. Parliamentarians and Royalists trading propaganda demonizing one another in the battle for religious superiority coupled with the anti-witch zealotry of Matthew Hopkins—the so-called Witchfinder General—set the stage for some 250 to 300 people to be accused of witchcraft. "Likewise, judicial and administrative structures, geared to supporting the war effort, were stretched sufficiently to dilute that caution which the assize courts normally demonstrated in matters of witchcraft," explains James Sharpe in "Witch Hunts in Britain." The only large-scale witch hunt on English soil saw the deaths of nearly 100 people thanks to Hopkins, which, in turn, influenced English colonial views about supernatural evil.

Midway through the lecture, I began to look around. The studs and zippers on my leather jacket clanked against the wooden pew, echoing loudly inside the spacious church. Everyone in attendance seemed to be at least a decade or more older—and dressed far more respectably. I was apprehensive about the coming ceremony and questioned if I belonged there. In a nearby row, a woman shifted in her seat, and her blouse lifted up to reveal a triple goddess tattoo. The familiar sight was reassuring. I supposed I was in the right place after all.

Although colonists in Connecticut had left their former country, they remained connected to the culture and politics of England. Those from the elite to the very poor all had networks of communication that snaked back to the Old World, including letters and books as well as pamphlets read aloud and gossip spread in bedrooms and over kitchen tables. "The emphasis on witches and the invective language used in pamphlets, broadsides and sermons provided a highly charged atmosphere," explains Richard Ross in *Before Salem: Witch Hunting in the Connecticut River Valley, 1647–1663*, which "stimulated an atmosphere receptive to the witch hunts in New England in the period under discussion."

Connecticut winters were harsh, and the threat of disease, famine, and conflict with "heathen" tribes stoked fears of demonic forces at work. This was only made worse by ministers declaring the Devil to be alive and active in this unforgiving new land. Acts of *maleficium* abounded, and "witchcraft was a continuous presence in the life of local communities," John Demos writes in *Entertaining Satan: Witchcraft and the Culture of Early New England*. "Trials were usually preceded by months or years of preparation, during which suspicion intensified and spread, gossip flourished, relations between accused and accusers gradually deteriorated." Sometimes, revenge was a dish served freezing cold.

Alice or Alse Young was the first woman executed for witchcraft in New England. She had moved to Windsor, Connecticut, from London with her ailing husband in 1640/1 and was believed to be a cunning woman or have some knowledge of healing that her community found threatening. Little evidence remains about what exactly she did to invoke the ire of Windsor, but Young was hanged as a witch in Hartford in 1647. Her daughter, also named Alice, would be accused of witchcraft too, some thirty years later.

Witchcraft was built into Connecticut law, and church and state were intimately entwined from the start. The 1642 *Capital Laws of Connecticut* modeled after the *Massachusetts Body of Liberties* from the year prior included a witchcraft statute crafted from three biblical passages, including "thou shalt not suffer a witch to live." To execute said laws, legal manuals written in England were brought over to serve as guides. Michael Dalton's *Countrey Justice*, published four years after the Lancashire witch trials ended, was an important tool for New England courts. "Dalton's book came to function much like the third part of the *Malleus Maleficarum* or *Witches' Hammer* had earlier on the continent," Ross affirms.

The second person to be hanged for witchcraft in Hartford bears all the marks of the sexually transgressive witch—and was deemed a worthy subject for noted Puritan minister Cotton Mather to mention in his book *Magnalia Christi Americana*.

Mary Johnson was an unmarried servant accused of stealing from her employer's household and was whipped as punishment. Sometime later, Mary was accused of witchcraft and confessed that the Devil did favors for her. When she was scolded for not cleaning the soot out of her master's chimney one day, the Devil came along and helped clear the hearth. When she was sent to wrangle her master's hogs, the Devil helped her do that, too. Mary also confessed to the "murder of a child," and admitted she was guilty of "uncleanness with men and Devils." Later records suggest that she was pregnant at the time of her conviction. Mary Johnson was allowed to give birth in prison before they slipped the noose around her neck.

I learned more horrifying stories of women punished for merely trying to survive under exceedingly harsh conditions. But under patriarchal Puritanism, such women were easy scapegoats to shore up community obedience and piety. When the lecture came to a close, a constellation of names and questions hung in the air. A hush fell upon the room as Reverend Rochelle A. Stackhouse stepped up to her pulpit to deliver an impassioned sermon about the legacy of the witch hunts.

Drawing from Psalm 43, Stackhouse affirmed "the need for truth-telling," in the planning of this ceremony. She spoke of contemporary persecutions and the necessity for vigilance on the part of everyone in this country to do what we can to stop oppression of all kinds. (I had noticed a rainbow flag affixed to the church when I walked up.) The reverend instructed those present to pick up a black stone from a basket near the entrance doors and head outside to the garden. Inspired by the Scottish tradition, these *cairn* stones would be piled together by our hands as a memorial to those who were not allowed to be buried here when they were executed as witches.

"We are going to allow them to rest in our sacred ground," announced Stackhouse. The small group filed outside into the garden with solemnity, slowly stacking each stone on a square of dirt between plantings. Then, we were asked to close our eyes and pray to whatever was holy to us. The reverend's voice was rich and clear and strong, asking forgiveness for the sins and faults of the church that once persecuted these women. "We grieve the loss of our ancestors," she intoned as the group was enrapt in collective prayer. She asked that we all have the strength to prevent the othering and persecution of people today who are in the same position these "witches" once were. "Our society excels at persecuting people as Other," the reverend said, but asked us again to commit ourselves "to seek understanding and community with all."

The names of the accused eleven witches were read aloud. I squeezed my eyes shut to keep tears from springing forth. The air hummed with "amen" and "blessed be" before the group dispersed into the afternoon sun.

Next door to the church, I found remnants of the accused in front of the Ancient Burying Ground. The oldest cemetery in Hartford was awash in gold, scarlet, and green leaves. Nearby bricks surrounding a statue of Reverend Samuel Stone—who played a pivotal role in Connecticut's witch trials—have been marked as memorials. One reads: "Alse Young CT Witch Hanged May 26, 1647." Nearby is another: "Mary Barnes Hanged 1662/3 For Witchcraft."

I stepped gingerly over the bricks into the Ancient Burying Ground. Winged skulls chiseled into aging gravestones were in stark contrast to the vivid colors above and below. I explored the historical graves of former witch accusers, ministers, and magistrates—the only ones involved in the witch trials dignified with a final resting place. I overheard some of the attendees speaking about other witch trial memorials in process across Connecticut as I walked past the memorial garden.

Through the wrought-iron fence, I could see the small pyramid of black cairn stones we had just left. Falling leaves had already obscured part of the pile, but no more than the history of Connecticut's witch hunts had already been obscured.

It's easy to be cynical about honoring eleven long-dead people when so many continue to suffer in the United States today, singled out as targets by religious leaders and politicians alike. But the care with which the reverend tended to the long-forgotten members of her flock was moving. Who would have thought that witches would be the thing to finally bring Pagans and Christians together in ritual and prayer.

HALLOWEEN IN WITCH CITY

Salem, Massachusetts

*Handmaidens of the Lord should go so as to distinguish themselves
from Handmaidens of the Devil.*

—Cotton Mather

SALEM WAS A GHOST TOWN ON Devil's Night. I trekked through the
soaked grounds of Salem Common in the dark, not a soul in sight. Red
lights burst like flames from the windows of a stately home across the
street. The Salem Witch Museum lurched into the night sky next door,
turning shades of blue and green and purple. A lone man appeared,
stumbling in circles toward me, deeply drunk or perhaps deep in ritual.
I wielded my umbrella like a shield, hoping he would take his presence
elsewhere. He hovered nearby in uncomfortable, wobbly silence before
disappearing into the abyssal borders of the park.

Just then, there was movement in the gazebo at the center of the
common. A man in clerical robes towered over a woman in street clothes.
They seemed to be in the middle of some sacred rite, as if he were ini-
tiating her into something terrible. At least that's what my imagination

conjured up as I passed the two strangers. They became sinister statues in the domed platform, as the costumed man held the woman's face in his hands and kissed it, uncannily slow, no one around to witness the bizarre scene but me.

A thick mist twisted through the trees. The carnival booths ready for the next day's Halloween festivities were slick with rain, the glow of string lights overhead melting into orange and yellow leaves shivering in the wind. The city I traveled so far to see was nearly empty, and the sinister lore of Salem was getting to me. I wasn't frightened by supernatural evil or the lure of Satan's sweet embrace in the woods, though. It was the threat of everyday men, drunk on power or just plain drunk that sent me hurrying back to my Airbnb that night. They were the real danger in Salem centuries ago. After all, the most frightening part of the witch hunts has never been the fantastic lore about the Devil and his minions, but the evil that men do.

The next morning the rain came in undulating sheets. Branches did backbends in the squall. Despite nature's screams, Salem slowly came to life for its most hallowed day.

Halloween has roots in the fiery harvest festivals of Europe like Samhain, the Celtic celebration of "summer's end" and a time of death and rebirth in preparation for the cold, dark half of the year. Samhain is thought to be when the separation between the living and the dead—the veil—is the thinnest. For contemporary Pagans, it remains an occasion to honor those who no longer walk among us (the Catholic holidays All Saints' Day and All Souls' Day are roughly the same time), and many practitioners provide offerings to their ancestors—like those of Mexican heritage do on Día de los Muertos.

Things are never what they seem on Halloween. Our masks become more visible, and we reveal more of ourselves—both literally and figuratively—through the costumes we choose to wear. For twenty-four hours, identity is a category in disarray. Intimates become unrecognizable; strangers become fast friends. This carnivalesque atmosphere is only heightened in Salem, setting up potential scares at every corner and the option to channel forbidden energies you wouldn't dare to at home.

Caught in a reverie about the sacred and profane ways we celebrate this transitional part of fall, I ducked into a side street to get some respite from the fast-growing crowd. It was afternoon, and the weather was humid and wet like a fog machine was malfunctioning somewhere. I narrowly avoided a fanged clown, a trio of *Hocus Pocus* drag queens, and Jack Skellington on stilts only to find myself in the company of a small black cat, rubbing up against the brick facade of the Old Town Hall.

She was a liminal creature, like all of her kind. She could easily have been a consort of goddesses or Satanic star of supernatural affairs, like the black cat Tituba confessed she encountered in 1692 that said, "serve me."

Taken with this visitor, I followed her as she padded across the cobblestones of Essex Street. Her tail undulated in the air, becoming a hypnotic pendulum that coaxed me into an imagined past. She finally settled in front of a seafood restaurant down the street—not unusual fare for a cat—but in a flick of her vertical pupils we were in some other place—or, rather, some other time.

Apple trees were everywhere. Unpicked specimens littered the ground, their protective skins pulled apart by insects and small animals, leaving their browning flesh exposed to the elements. A figure moved through the orchard back into a wooden house, her gait brisk. There were noises inside, glass shattered. A man roared "Bridget!" and a woman's screams echoed through the rafters as the sound of flesh met flesh. She ran outside, her face bleeding.

The cat beckoned me to watch, clawing at my calves to keep me in place. Seasons turned, the trees withered, and Bridget's face turned shades of blue and green and purple as snow kissed the outstretched boughs around her home. The sounds in the house continued, forcing Bridget in and out of court as neighbors lodged complaints. He hit her; she hit back. She deemed him "old devil" with every blow and ended up in court again for coarse language. She was forced to sit out in the town square, mouth gagged, with her foul offense written on a piece of paper fastened to her forehead. And then one summer, the fighting stopped.

I watched Bridget prepare herself for the silent funeral and scrub her home of every trace of his violent musk. His land and his livestock were hers, but she had debts to pay and there would be little time to enjoy these new riches. Soon enough, she was accused of witchcraft, of appearing as a spectral black cat. Later, she was accused of theft. A lack of evidence saved her, but she was now marked with a heretical stain.

The harvests came and went and came, and only a few years later, Bridget was back in court. Now remarried to a woodcutter, she was accused of bewitching Abigail Williams, Mercy Lewis, Elizabeth Hubbard, Mary Walcott, and Ann Putnam Jr. The young girls were tormented by unseen evil, beset with terrors that drove them into fits. Demoniacs? Casualties of conversion disorder? Perpetrators of petty revenge on a power trip? Whatever the case may be, witchcraft was the diagnosis, and Bridget Bishop was a suspect.

I stood in the middle of the street, unbothered by people pouring around me. I saw Bridget's day in court in the old courthouse. She climbed to the second floor to face a reckoning with a town that didn't care a lick for her life. Witness after witness testified against Bishop, saying she tried to force them to sign the Devil's book, that she hit a child with a spade, that poppets stuck with pins were found in the walls of her home. They said she killed her first husband. They found a "preternatural teat" when they searched her trembling body. "I know nothing of it. I am innocent to a witch. I know not what a witch is," was all she could manage. But even though a second examination failed to find that same bit of flesh, she was the first to fall victim to the hangman's noose.

I was jostled back to the present by a crowd of tourists in costume, cackling and hooting. The cat became a phantom itch around my ankles. There was no courthouse, no Bridget, save for a play reenacting her trial—*Cry Innocent*—that was about to begin, mere steps from where her orchard once stood.

Halloween in Salem is witch tourism at its finest. Visiting the city at any other time of year doesn't make nearly as much as sense once you see jack-o'-lanterns lit and leering at you from local homes and shop windows, the streets shut down, overrun with costumed revelers, and incensed Christians protesting and proselytizing in front of the bronze *Bewitched* statue amid the crowd. The number of witch-hatted heads bobbing along the cobblestones increases exponentially, and witchcraft shops can barely contain the droves of gawkers and curious dabblers who mix in with the practicing witches in search of books, candles, oils, or burnables for their own celebrations.

It's a confusing mix of supernatural and historical lore that draws people to Salem throughout the year. The numerous museums, tours, plays, and merchandise reflect this ambivalence. Misinformation abounds—as it often does when witches are the subject in question—so "Witch City" has become a microcosm of the ways Western culture conflates and confuses ideas about witches and witchcraft.

Salem was the site of America's most infamous witch hunt in 1692, but those "witches" being hunted were merely women and men caught up in a frenzy driven by a mystery illness, intercommunity conflict, Puritanical zeal, and a broken justice system. The backdrop to all this? Eldritch darkness of the material and spiritual kind.

"In isolated settlements, in smoky, fire-lit homes, New Englanders lived very much in the dark," Stacy Schiff writes of Salem in *The New Yorker*, "where one listens more acutely, feels most passionately, and imagines most vividly, where the sacred and the occult thrive."

During the frigid winter between 1691 and 1692, two prepubescent girls in Reverend Samuel Parris's household began to exhibit signs of an unexplainable illness or, rather, they fell into "fits." At times they would be lifeless and still—all but dead to the world—then suddenly crescendo into violent cries and howl as if pinched and bitten by unseen entities. Upon multiple examinations, it was determined the reverend's daughter and niece, Elizabeth Parris and Abigail Williams, had been bewitched.

A growing number of girls began to exhibit the same symptoms across Salem Village, and the first three accusations were unleashed against Sarah Good, Sarah Osborne, and Tituba. Good was a beggar known for unruly, aggressive speech; Osborne was an outcast who rarely attended church; Tituba was an enslaved woman Reverend Parris had brought from Barbados. Under questioning—and, likely, physical aggression—Tituba confessed to a meeting with the Devil, saying that Good and Osborne were indeed witches and many more lurked in Salem, too.

As the group of afflicted accusers grew, so did the number of accused witches. The town was in such a state of upheaval that the Court of Oyer and Terminer, which had been convened in Salem Town to oversee the case, began to throw procedure out the window. "In Salem, the usual standards of evidence in New England courts had been abandoned for a time," explains Robert W. Thurston in *The Routledge History of Witchcraft*, "due to a strong sense that a conspiracy by evil forces against the good people was at work."

Dozens were accused of witchcraft based on spectral evidence—Bridget Bishop included. The possessed girls blamed Bridget for sending her specter to attack them, and a male neighbor accused Bishop of sending her spirit form to terrorize him in bed at night. Rebecca Nurse, an elderly grandmother, was also accused by the girls of afflicting them with her specter and "urging them to sign the devil's book." Nurse was later convicted and hanged, too. Martha Carrier would suffer the same fate, charged by the same possessed cadre of causing harm with her ghostly apparition. (They also revealed Carrier was told by the Devil "she should be Queen of Hell"—a plumb position indeed.)

Just as in Europe, the accused in Salem were predominately women. "Puritan belief made it easy to hold women responsible for the failures of the emerging economic system," writes Carol F. Karlsen in *The Devil in the Shape of a Woman: Witchcraft in Colonial New England*. She explains that the Puritan clergy had long fostered the idea that "if anyone were to blame for their troubles it was the daughters of Eve."

There were other reflections of old-world witch hunts in Salem, too. Englishman Michael Dalton's *Countrey Justice* was in use across the Eastern Seaboard, and the legal manual affirmed that the testimony of the afflicted or bewitched—including that of children—was admissible evidence in cases of witchcraft. In his manual, Dalton references nine-year-old Jennet Device supposedly speaking truth to power about Malkin Tower.

Cotton Mather, the Puritan minister who consulted on the Salem trials and who crafted multiple sermons and publications on the subject, also had a grandfather born in Lancashire. Mather had been told of the Pendle witch trials growing up and compared the incident to the one at hand in *The Wonders of the Invisible World*. When Mather delves into the case of minister George Burroughs, one of the few men to hang for witchcraft in Salem, he writes: "When the Lancashire Witches were condemn'd, I don't Remember that there was any considerable further

Evidence, than that of the Bewitched, and then that of some that confessed." Although torture wasn't technically legal under Massachusetts code, as in Lancashire, the appalling conditions of the jails and callous interrogation methods applied to the accused remain highly suspect. (There's more on that subject at the Witch Dungeon Museum.)

By the end of 1692, well over 150 people had been accused and dozens had undergone trial when Governor William Phips forcibly concluded the craze. Fourteen women, five men, and two dogs had been hanged, and one man had been tortured to death with heavy rocks. A few more people died in prison. Within the following years, Reverend Parris, a judge, and members of the jury involved in the case would express deep regret at the outcome of the trials. It became Salem's greatest shame.

For centuries after the end of the Salem witch trials, writers, philosophers, artists, and politicians alike would appropriate the story for their own devices—most notably Arthur Miller. Though many Americans take his 1953 play *The Crucible* as a documentation of what happened in Salem, it is in no way historically accurate and best understood as a polemic criticizing Cold War McCarthyism. While Miller and his ilk were busy twisting history to create great art, scholars were hard at work trying to uncover the exact motives for Salem's witch hunt. Stacy Schiff details a laundry list of causes that historians have come up with in *The Witches: Salem, 1692*. She writes:

> Our first true-crime story has been attributed to generational, sexual, economic, ecclesiastical, and class tensions; regional hostilities imported from England; food poisoning; a hothouse religion in a cold climate; teenage hysteria; fraud, taxes, conspiracy; political instability; trauma induced by Indian attacks; and to witch-craft itself.

Scholars still disagree about what exactly happened in 1692. Robert W. Thurston suggests that Salem hysteria was "above all the problem of evidence during a panic, not any broader streams of thought or economic development that produced the Salem witch hunt." However, he does recognize that Indian attacks, sexism in early modern society, and additional local issues "sharpened suspicion that Satan was on the scene."

Others continue to offer alternate readings of New England's most haunting debacle.

Salem was the place where the witch's body was irrevocably politicized in North America. Because of Salem, "witch hunt" remains a potent political firebomb—and frequently misused metaphor—in the contemporary United States. The fact that there is no single, universally agreed-upon narrative of the Salem witch trials can be frustrating, but makes them endlessly fascinating. Such is the allure of Salem, a beloved destination for travelers hell-bent on miring themselves in history, myth, witchcraft, and mystery.

I went in and out of shops, museums, and memorials, trying to make sense of Salem. In the buildings on Essex Street, ghosts, witches, and pumpkins peered out of every glass orifice. Neck crooked beneath an umbrella in full costume, I was a Satanic chorus member of *Cats* in desperate need of a hair dryer. Droplets splattered in all directions as I passed books excavating Salem's past and witchy merch that ran the gamut from charming to uncomfortably tacky. (The "I Got Stoned in Salem" shirt, a gruesome play on Giles Cory's death by pressing, gave me pause.) Nearby, I saw a Hawthorne vs. Poe sign in a window, pitting Salem's greatest novelist against another master of the macabre. (The house Nathaniel Hawthorne made famous, the House of the Seven Gables, is still an eerie must-see.) I was equally taken by the various mundane bits of infrastructure emblazoned with witches on broom-stick—police cars, water towers—that have been transformed into sights in their own right.

The somber side of Salem is just as compelling. Visitors can find a memorial for those hanged and tortured to death next to Salem's Bury-ing Point cemetery in an enclosure of twenty benches dedicated to each victim. Some of these victims' partial last words are chiseled into stone beneath your feet as you enter, an apt metaphor for their silencing. A ten-minute drive takes you to the location of the gallows at Proctor's Ledge, where another memorial was erected in 2016 to those hanged there. Due northwest is the Witchcraft Victim's Memorial across from the site of the Salem Village Meeting House where many examina-tions took place, as well as the Rebecca Nurse Homestead. Both are in Danvers, the former site of Salem Village. The sprawling grounds of the homestead feature an 1885 memorial—arguably the first Salem witch trials attraction—which was built to honor Nurse long after death.

But what of witchcraft? For Salem today is far more than a site of murder, persecution, and fun-house spooks. It is also the home of many practicing witches.

In 1970, TV's bounciest, blondest, and most benign witch, Saman-tha Stephens, hung her pointed hat here in several *Bewitched* episodes (hence the statue on Essex and Washington), but it was Official Witch of Salem Laurie Cabot who ignited Salem's witchcraft revival when she opened her first witchcraft shop in 1971. Some fifty years later, Salem is overflowing with witchcraft as much as it is witch history. There's the yearly Psychic Fair and Witches Market, Salem Witches' Hal-loween Ball, Olde Salem Village Dark Arts Night Faire, and a pan-oply of stores offering all kinds of books, services, and classes. Some establishments explicitly reference Salem's past—Hex: Old World Witchery sells Bridget Bishop poppets and The Cauldron Black offers courses that delve into historical folk magic traditions. Other shops do so implicitly—HausWitch harnesses the intersection of politics and witchcraft in its intersectional feminist wares and workshops.

After dark, Halloween reached fever pitch across Salem. The sky was blackened violet and people were proudly blood-dripping, wig-wearing, and pentagram-clad. I decided to push past my fear of crowds and step full force into the maelstrom for a walking tour.

As with every attraction in Salem, there are so many options it's hard to know what to choose—but healthy skepticism is always a good place to start. I chose a tour equally enamored with skepticism: the Satanic Salem Walking Tour. Crafted and led by veteran tour guide, practicing witch, and historian Thomas O'Brien Vallor, the walk is affiliated with The Satanic Temple and takes you through Salem both real and imagined. Witty, irreverent, and historically accurate, Satanic Salem draws important parallels between the witch trials and our contemporary political climate, warts and all.

Nimbly moving amid the throng of costumed revelers clogging every inch of the city, we learned about Salem's past and present. Like the best art and writing that have been spun from Salem's legacy, the Satanic Salem Walking Tour helps to unveil the destructive potential of Christian fundamentalism and unchecked governmental power. (It also underscores the many ways contemporary activists, feminists, Satanists, radicals, and rebels are fighting back against this scourge in the present.) In between stops, Vallor offered up withering bon mots like "We should be called the hysteria city, not the Witch City" or "the Puritans were the Taliban of Christianity." Fog hung specter-like in the unseasonably warm night as the group kept moving, the wind whipping my hair into Whitesnake video heights.

Two and a half hours later, the walking tour ended near the Old Town Hall. Our guide graciously answered questions from the group about witchcraft (all witches aren't Wiccan!), Satanism (it's not just Devil worship anymore, kids!), and local transportation (Uber on Halloween, are you kidding?) before disappearing into the night with a flourish. The streets remained alive with a teeming psychedelic congregation, drunk on booze and illusions. Halloween still had a hold on Salem.

I headed to the outskirts of town thinking of the dead that this holiday is supposed to memorialize and the ways in which their memories have been embraced and distorted in Witch City. Although I have visited many times, Salem always seems to remain just out of reach. Is it a haunted theme park? The witch industrial complex gone wild? A sacred site of cultural memory? A charming New England town? It is all these things—but more. Like so many cities with weighty history, Salem is a shape-shifter, becoming the place you want it to be when your feet are on the ground, when you walk among its people and parks and streets. Like the archetypal witch, Salem's magic lies in eluding simple characterizations.

RE-ENCHANTING TRAVEL

Brooklyn, New York

IN NEW YORK, WITCHES GROW thick and wild. There's a witch festival, art show, burlesque night, or street fair nearly every month in New York City, an entire Cornell University Library collection dedicated to witchcraft in Ithaca, and witch shops in Kingston, Albany, Syracuse, Buffalo, and beyond.

New York state has long been home to a host of esoteric practices, birthing Spiritualism in the "Burned-Over District" of western and central New York in the mid-nineteenth century. When the suffrage movement was gaining ground decades later in the same region, New York native Matilda Joslyn Gage was the first feminist to reclaim and rehabilitate the witch in her activism with the 1893 book *Woman, Church and State.*

In the early 1960s, Raymond Buckland brought the Wiccan religion from England to Long Island with founder Gerald Gardner's blessing, inspiring countless American witches in the process—and opening the Buckland Museum of Witchcraft and Magick in Bay

Shore. (The museum has since moved to Cleveland.) In 1968, New York City became the breeding ground for the witch-inspired guerrilla theater activist group WITCH (the Women's International Terrorist Conspiracy from Hell). And in 1970, Central Park was the backdrop for a "Witch-In."

Today, Manhattan boasts the city's oldest witch shop, Enchantments, and Brooklyn offers multiple feminist and social justice–minded witchcraft shops and community centers from Cult Party to Catland. But in the early modern era? Witches were few and far between.

Back when New York was part of a Dutch colony known as New Netherland, there is no evidence that witchcraft beliefs troubled the population. "The home land of the Dutch had, beyond all others, outgrown the panic," notes George Lincoln Burr in *Narratives of the New England Witchcraft Cases, 1648–1706*. But that changed when the territory came under English control. In 1665, Ralph and Mary Hall were accused of killing a man and his infant through witchcraft in Setauket. The two were brought to the court assizes in Manhattan at Fort James (where the Alexander Hamilton US Custom House now stands). The court found with typical gender bias that there was "nothing considerable to charge [Ralph] with," but there was some suspicion Mary was guilty. In the end, the authorities decided it was "nothing considerable of value to take away her life," so Ralph was tasked with posting a bond for his wife to ensure her good behavior. The two were released and nothing more came of the incident.

Perhaps the most dramatic witchcraft case within modern-day New York state occurred in the far reaches of Long Island in 1657. Back then, Elizabeth Garlick was a woman of East Hampton accused of bewitching a young mother to death. Over fifty and likely a French Huguenot, Garlick had knowledge of herbs and the healing arts but was distrusted by some in her community. (Neighbors reported she had a cat familiar and once used the evil eye to kill a newborn.) So when sixteen-year-old

Elizabeth Howell—daughter of the town's most powerful man Lion Gardiner—screamed out on her deathbed that a witch was overtaking her and named Goody Garlick as the culprit, few were surprised. Garlick was sent to Hartford for her trial where she wasn't convicted, but, similar to the Hall case, her husband had to post a bond to vouch for her continued good behavior. She lived out the rest of her life in East Hampton.

Inside the South End Burying Ground in East Hampton there are now occasional ghost tours at the historic cemetery that delve into the Garlick affair. Ducks float across a picturesque pond, and an old windmill looks out over the weathered headstones. (Lion Gardiner's medieval-style tomb is the most extravagant of the bunch.) Nearby is the East Hampton Historical Society for those who wish to delve deeper into early modern Long Island life.

Apart from these and a few other isolated incidents, many "witches" of New York actually came to the colony seeking asylum from witchcraft accusations in New England. My research revealed no significant witch memorials in New York state to speak of—except, maybe, in Brooklyn.

The final stop on my witch hunt was a homecoming. A short drive from my apartment, I found myself in the Brooklyn Museum at an installation designed to sacralize and pay tribute to female power and persecution—a subject you cannot tackle without mentioning the witch. Passing underneath six processional banners in bright reds, yellows, and oranges woven into pyramids, swirls, and zigzags, I read the initiatory words of the work aloud in a whisper. The final stanza hung in my heart as I entered a black shining triangle of a room. "And then everywhere was Eden once again . . ."

The Dinner Party is a 1978 installation by feminist art progenitor Judy Chicago featuring thirty-nine place settings at a triangular table dedicated to influential women of Western civilization. Beneath these plates is a "Heritage Floor" of porcelain tiles bearing the names of 999 mythical and historical women who support, reflect, and contextualize those featured above. It is an idyllic gathering, Edenic even—at least before the fall. For the biblical Eden was never a place for women who desired more than they were given. Like our witchy foremother Eve—and her dark sister Lilith—many of the women Chicago includes in her piece were demonized for their art, their ideas, or their actions.

Chicago was initially inspired by Leonardo da Vinci's *Last Supper* in the early stages of creation. "I imagined duplicating the number of persons represented in Leonardo's work, that is, thirteen," she writes in *The Dinner Party: Restoring Women to History*. "It occurred to me that this was the number of witches that make a coven, which seemed particularly interesting because, while men were considered holy, witches were perceived as the embodiment of female evil."

The thirteen place settings on the first wing make room for ancient feminine deities from the Primordial Goddess and the Fertile Goddess to Ishtar and Kali. The symbolism on the ceramic plates is vaginal and vivid; the accompanying chalice, fork, knife, spoon, and napkin exquisitely simple. Moving around to the second wing, I passed places for Saint Bridget, Trotula, and Christine de Pisan—all figures whose names arose in my research for *Witch Hunt*.

Now permanently on view at the Elizabeth A. Sackler Center for Feminist Art, *The Dinner Party* is a literal feast for the eyes. Over the years there have been some necessary critiques about the ways race, gender variance, and historicity are expressed in the work, but it remains an incredible feat of craftswomanship. Most importantly, *The Dinner Party* directly engages with memorializing the victims of the early modern witch hunts.

When I was interviewing *Waking the Witch* author Pam Grossman for *Witches, Sluts, Feminists*, she described the work to me as "a giant shrine to the divine feminine and feminist history" and "one of the most witchly art pieces that has ever been created." But *The Dinner Party* isn't witchly only because of its symbolism and its embracing of the divine feminine. One of the women with a seat at the table is an accused witch—as are many inscribed on the floor.

Seated between Hildegard of Bingen and Christine de Pisan, Petronilla de Meath is recognized by Chicago for being the first known woman to be burned at the stake for heresy in Ireland. Petronilla's plate is at once bell, book, cauldron, and candle in flaming orange against a backdrop of blue, deep purple, and white. The embroidered cloth runner underneath the plate includes knotted Celtic motifs surrounding a broom. On the floor, Alice Kyteler's name is scrawled in gold cursive, as are the names of Joan of Arc, Geillis Duncan, Agnes Sampson, Elizabeth Southerns, Anne Redfearne, Tituba, and over a dozen others. It reads like a list of characters within our current discussion.

"The figure of the witch mirrors—albeit sometimes in distorted form—the many images and self-images of feminism itself," proposes Diane Purkiss in *The Witch in History*. And in no other art work is this more apparent than *The Dinner Party*.

I spent as long as I could in Judy Chicago's dimly lit chapel. If it weren't for the guards, I would have poured wine into every one of the chalices as Pagan Communion, invoking a collective, syncretic prayer. I would have piled the plates high with pomegranates and apples, mandrake and belladonna, inviting snakes and spectral cats to twist around my ankles as these feminine figures joined me across the table, conjuring the force of the divine feminine and the fury of the demonic feminine that has been infused into the story of Western civilization, of witches and witchcraft, and of women for millennia.

It was a feminist fantasy that warmed me as I made my way back to my neighborhood. But before going home, I was moved to stop into Catland Books. Walking past an altar overflowing with idols and offerings, I picked a volume off the shelf as a curl of incense smoke arched overhead. In an act of spontaneous bibliomancy, I opened up a random page and began to read.

In *Communing with the Ancestors: Your Spirit Guides, Bloodline Allies, and the Cycle of Reincarnation*, Raven Grimassi waxes prophetic about ancestry and place. (I was hardly surprised the book I chose and the section I turned to were exactly the subject I was seeking.) Bringing up the concept of the "Living River of Blood," Grimassi explains that it is "an interfacing stream of energy that circulates" between you and your kin—their DNA to yours—from the dead to the living to the dead once more. "In the mystical sense, the River is where the Ancestors move to meet us," he writes, noting that "it is not their realm, but a conveyance we envision as a river." Grimassi then affirms that one way to connect with the dead—and, thus the past—is through place, revealing that "the spirits of the Dead can become the spirits of the land, transformed into *genius loci*."

I slipped the book back onto the shelf, turning Grimassi's words over in my mind. Our blood link to the past flows across continents, cultures, and epochs. If our ancestors can become part of the land, a place can hold as much of our heritage as a person. I replayed the encounters I had with forests, mountains, rivers, and old oak trees; with churches, crumbling buildings, and cemeteries. In my travels, I was drawn to places near where I knew my ancestors had lived. When I was quiet enough, open enough, I caught glimpses of them in my breath on a cold, clear day, in the flames of a bonfire, the ripple of a wave.

"In rediscovering land spirits, we cannot help but notice their modernity," writes Claude Lecouteux in *Demons and Spirits of the Land*.

"They guided our ancestors to respect their environment. . . . In order to prosper, then, we must continue to honor the *genii loci*." And by honoring the *genii loci*, we can honor our ancestors, too.

We live in a disenchanted world now, or so it's been said. Magic is no longer a technology of the mainstream. Superstition and religion have been tempered by science. But those who desire to transcend the rational confines of reality can still do so in travel.

When traveling, it is easy to find the sacred in the everyday—in the way flowers perfume the breeze, voices echo across cobblestones, and the sun sets in a hallowed site. When traveling, so much more feels enspirited and ensouled, electric and alive.

"We travel, some of us forever, to seek other states, other lives, other souls," wrote Anais Nin. And it's no coincidence that the language of travel is the language of magic: offering seekers transportive access to other worlds through their whims and will alone.

Centuries ago, witches were the aspirational jet-setters. Who but the witch could fly from one place to the next, freely traversing cities and countrysides, forests and mountaintops—or never leave her bed at all but venturing far and wide all the same? Now, travel is a form of modern magic, a potent way to tap into the powers of the archetypal witch.

If travel can be magic, it can also be witchcraft. For travel, too, is a practice that shifts perceptions, makes connections, and alters reality itself. To view travel through this enchanted lens imbues both travel and traveler with radical potential. And what we do with our potential matters. In a sense, travel has made witches of us all. By re-enchanting travel, we may in the process re-enchant our world.

TRAVEL RESOURCES

France

Paris

BIBLIOTHÈQUE NATIONALE

Site Richelieu
58, rue de Richelieu
75002 Paris, France
bnf.fr/en/richelieu

CONCIERGERIE

2 Boulevard du Palais
75001 Paris, France
paris-conciergerie.fr

HÔTEL-DE-VILLE

Place de l'Hôtel de Ville
75004 Paris, France

LOUVRE MUSEUM

Rue de Rivoli
75001 Paris, France
louvre.fr/en

Notre-Dame de Paris

6 Parvis Notre-Dame Pl. Jean-Paul II
75004 Paris, France

Père Lachaise

8 Boulevard de Ménilmontant
75020 Paris, France

Rouen

Church of Saint Joan of Arc

Place du Vieux-Marché
76000 Rouen, France

Church of Saint Ouen

Place du Général de Gaulle
76000 Rouen, France

Historial Jeanne d'Arc

7 Rue Saint-Romain
76000 Rouen, France
historial-jeannedarc.fr

La Cabine

109 Rue Ganterie
76000 Rouen, France
jeanneadit.com

Tower of Joan of Arc

Rue Bouvreuil
76000 Rouen, France

Germany

Bamberg

Bamberg Tourismus & Kongress Service

Geyerswörthstraße 5
96047 Bamberg, Germany
"Death by Fire and the Hammer of the Witches" tour
en.bamberg.info

Old Town Hall

Obere Brücke
96047 Bamberg, Germany

Saint Hedwig Apotheke

Franz-Ludwig-Straße 7
96047 Bamberg, Germany

Schönleinsplatz

96047 Bamberg, Germany

ZEILER HEXENTURM

Obere Torstraße 14
97475 Zeil am Main, Germany
zeiler-hexenturm.de

Harz Mountains

BROCKENHAUS MUSEUM

Brockenplateau
38879 Wernigerode, Germany
brockenhaus-harz.de

HARZER SCHMALSPURBAHN BAHNHOF WERNIGERODE-WESTERNTOR

Unter den Zindeln 3
38855 Wernigerode, Germany
hsb-wr.de

HARZEUM

Hexentanzplatz 3
06502 Thale, Germany

OBSCURUM THALE

Bahnhofstraße 1
06502 Thale, Germany
obscurum-thale.de

QUEDLINBURG RATHAUS

Markt 1
06484 Quedlinburg, Germany

TEUFELSMAUER

06502 Thale, Germany

Ireland

KILKENNY CASTLE

The Parade, Collegepark
Kilkenny, Ireland
kilkennycastle.ie

KYTELER'S INN

27 Saint Kieran's St., Gardens
Kilkenny, Ireland
kytelersinn.com

MEDIEVAL MILE MUSEUM

2 Saint Mary's Ln., High St., Collegepark
Kilkenny, R95 ANW5, Ireland
medievalmilemuseum.ie

Petronella

Butter Slip Ln., Gardens
Kilkenny, Ireland
petronella.ie

Saint Canice's Cathedral & Round Tower

The Close, Coach Rd.
Kilkenny, Ireland
stcanicescathedral.ie

Italy

Capannori

Oak of the Witches

Villa Carrara
San Martino in Colle
55012 Capannori, Italy

Florence

Baptistery of San Giovanni

Piazza San Giovanni
50122 Florence, Italy

Gelateria Artigianale la Strega Nocciola

Ponte Vecchio
Via de' Bardi, 51r
50125 Florence, Italy

La Soffitta delle Streghe

Via Romana, 135r
50125 Florence, Italy

Palazzo Vecchio

Piazza della Signoria
50122 Florence, Italy
musefirenze.it

San Miniato al Monte

Via delle Porte Sante, 34
50125 Florence, Italy

Sant'Ambrogio

Via Giosuè Carducci, 1
50121 Florence, Italy

Uffizi Gallery

Piazzale degli Uffizi, 6
50122 Florence, Italy
uffizi.it

Genoa

Palazzo Ducale

Piazza Giacomo Matteotti, 9
16123 Genoa, Italy
visitgenoa.it

Porto Venere

CHURCH OF SAINT PETER

Lungo Calata Doria
19025 Porto Venere, Italy

Riola

MUSEO INTERNAZIONALE DEI TAROCCHI

Via Arturo Palmieri, 5/1 Riola
40038 Vergato, Italy
museodeitarocchi.net

Siena

BASILICA OF SAN DOMENICO

Piazza San Domenico, 1
53100 Siena, Italy

PIAZZA DEL CAMPO

Il Campo
53100 Siena, Italy

SIENA DUOMO

Piazza del Duomo, 8
53100 Siena, Italy

Triora

Museo Etnostorico della Stregoneria

Piazza Tommaso Beato Reggio
18010 Triora, Italy

Museo di Triora Etnografico e della Stregoneria

Corso Italia 1
18010 Triora, Italy
museotriora.it

San Bernardino Church

18010 Triora, Italy

Vatican City

The Vatican

00120 Vatican City, Italy
vatican.va
museivaticani.va

United Kingdom

Cornwall

The Museum of Witchcraft and Magic

The Harbour
Boscastle
Cornwall PL35 0HD
United Kingdom
museumofwitchcraftandmagic.co.uk

Edinburgh

Edinburgh Castle

Castlehill
Edinburgh EH1 2NG
United Kingdom

National Museum of Scotland

Chambers Street
Edinburgh EH1 1JF
United Kingdom
nms.ac.uk

Palace of Holyrood House

Canongate
Edinburgh EH8 8DX
United Kingdom
rct.uk

The Witchery by the Castle

352 Castlehill
Edinburgh EH1 2NF
United Kingdom
thewitchery.com

The Witches' Well

555 Castlehill
Edinburgh EH1 2ND
United Kingdom

Lancashire

Alice Nutter memorial statue

Roughlee
Nelson BB9 6NS
United Kingdom

Clitheroe Castle

Castle Hill
Clitheroe BB7 1BA
United Kingdom

Lancaster Castle

Castle Grove
Lancaster LA1 1YJ
United Kingdom
lancastercastle.com

Pendle Heritage Center

Colne Rd., Barrowford
Burnley BB9 6JQ
United Kingdom
pendleheritage.co.uk

Saint Mary's Church

5 Cross Ln., Newchurch-in-Pendle
Burnley BB12 9JR
United Kingdom
stmarysnewchurchinpendle.org.uk

Samlesbury Hall

Preston New Rd., Samlesbury
Preston PR5 0UP
United Kingdom
samlesburyhall.co.uk

Witches Galore

14 Newchurch Village, Newchurch-in-Pendle
Burnley BB12 9JR
United Kingdom
witchesgalore.co.uk

London

The Atlantis Bookshop

49A Museum St., Holborn
London WC1A 1LY
United Kingdom
theatlantisbookshop.com

The British Museum

Great Russell St., Bloomsbury
London WC1B 3DG
United Kingdom
britishmuseum.org

Chelsea Physic Garden

66 Royal Hospital Rd., Chelsea
London SW3 4HS
United Kingdom
chelseaphysicgarden.co.uk

The Mandrake Hotel

20-21 Newman St., Fitzrovia
London W1T 1PG
United Kingdom
themandrake.com

Treadwell's Books

33 Store St., Fitzrovia
London WC1E 7BS
United Kingdom
treadwells-london.com

Tyburn Tree

Tyburnia
London W1H 7EL
United Kingdom

North Berwick

Saint Andrew's Old Kirk

27 Victoria Rd.
North Berwick EH39 4JL
United Kingdom

Nottingham

Haunted Happenings and Spooky Nights

Parklands Connexion
Stanhope St.
Long Eaton
Pendle Witch Weekend ghost hunt
hauntedhappenings.co.uk

CRESWELL CRAGS MUSEUM AND HERITAGE CENTRE

Crags Road
Welbeck, Worksop
Nottinghamshire S80 3LH
Witch Mark tourc
creswell-crags.org.uk

SHERWOOD FOREST

Edwinstowe
Nottinghamshire NG21 9RN
visitsherwood.co.uk

United States

Connecticut

ANCIENT BURYING GROUND

60 Gold St.
Hartford, CT 06103
theancientburyingground.org

CENTER CHURCH: FIRST CHURCH OF CHRIST

60 Gold St.
Hartford, CT 06103
centerchurchhartford.org

Delaware

REHOBOTH BEACH ANNUAL SEA WITCH FESTIVAL

501 Rehoboth Avenue
Rehoboth Beach, DE 19971
beach-fun.com

ZWAANENDAEL MUSEUM

102 Kings Highway
Lewes, DE 19958
history.delaware.gov

Maryland

HISTORIC ST. MARY'S CITY

18751 Hogaboom Lane
St. Mary's City, MD 20686
hsmcdigshistory.org

Massachusetts

BEWITCHED STATUE

235 Essex St.
Salem, MA 01970

THE BURYING POINT

Charter St.
Salem, MA 01970

The Cauldron Black

65 Wharf Street
Salem, MA 01970
thecauldronblack.com

Cry Innocent

32 Derby Sq.
Salem, MA 01970
historyalivesalem.com

HausWitch Home + Healing

144 Washington St.
Salem, MA 01970
hauswitchstore.com

Hex: Old World Witchery

246 Essex St.
Salem, MA 01970
hexwitch.com

The House of the Seven Gables

115 Derby Street
Salem, MA 01970
7gables.org

The Olde Salem Village Dark Arts Night Faire

Salem Pioneer Village
98 West Avenue
Salem, MA 01970
blackveilstudio.com

Proctor's Ledge Memorial

7 Pope St.
Salem, MA 01970

Rebecca Nurse Homestead

149 Pine St.
Danvers, MA 01923
rebeccanurse.org

The Salem Psychic Fair and Witches' Market

Witch City Mall
1 Church Street
Salem, MA 01970
festivalofthedead.com

Salem Witch Museum

19 1/2 N. Washington Square
Salem, MA 01970
salemwitchmuseum.com

Salem Witch Trials Memorial

24 Liberty St.
Salem, MA 01970

The Salem Witches' Halloween Ball

Hawthorne Hotel
18 Washington Square West
festivalofthedead.com

Satanic Salem Walking Tour

Derby Square
Salem, MA 01970
satanictours.com

Witch Dungeon Museum

16 Lynde St.
Salem, MA 01970
witchdungeon.com

Witchcraft Victim's Memorial

172 Hobart St.
Danvers, MA 01923

New York

THE BROOKLYN MUSEUM

Elizabeth A. Sackler Center for Feminist Art
200 Eastern Pkwy.
Brooklyn, NY 11238
brooklynmuseum.org

CATLAND BOOKS

987 Flushing Ave.
Brooklyn, NY 11206
catlandbooks.com

THE CORNELL UNIVERSITY WITCHCRAFT COLLECTION

Carl A. Kroch Library
216 East Ave.
Ithaca, NY 14850
ebooks.library.cornell.edu

CULT PARTY

53 Waterbury St.
Brooklyn, NY 11206
cultpartynyc.com

East Hampton Historical Society

101 Main St.
East Hampton, NY 11937
easthamptonhistory.org

Enchantments

424 E. 9th St.
New York, NY 10009
enchantmentsincnyc.com

Lily Dale Museum

16-18 Library St.
Lily Dale, NY 14752
lilydaleassembly.org

Matilda Joslyn Gage Foundation and Museum

210 E. Genesee St.
Fayetteville, NY 13066
matildajoslyngage.org

South End Cemetery

34 James Ln.
East Hampton, NY 11937

Ohio

Buckland Museum of Witchcraft and Magick

2155 Broadview Road
Cleveland, OH 44109
bucklandmuseum.org

Pennsylvania

Pennsbury Manor

400 Pennsbury Memorial Road
Morrisville, PA 19067
pennsburymanor.org

Virginia

Colonial Williamsburg

101 Visitor Center Dr.
Williamsburg, VA 23185
colonialwilliamsburg.org

Grace Sherwood Statue

4520-4540 N. Witchduck Rd.
Virginia Beach, VA 23455

Historic Jamestowne

1368 Colonial Pkwy.
Jamestown, VA 23081
historicjamestowne.org

Jamestown Settlement

2110 Jamestown Rd.
Williamsburg, VA 23185
historyisfun.org

Old Donation Episcopal Church

The Historic Church
4449 N. Witchduck Rd.
Virginia Beach, VA 23455

BIBLIOGRAPHY

Alighieri, Dante. *The Divine Comedy of Dante Alighieri: Inferno*. Robert Durling, trans. London: Oxford University Press, 1996.

Almond, Philip C. *The Devil: A New Biography*. Ithaca, NY: Cornell University Press, 2014.

———. *The Lancashire Witches: A Chronicle of Sorcery and Death on Pendle Hill*. London: I.B. Tauris, 2012.

Apps, Lara. *Male Witches in Early Modern Europe*. Manchester, UK: Manchester University Press, 2003.

"A Stroll in the Harz." *London Society*. June 1880: 568–572. *ProQuest*. Web. Aug. 22, 2019.

Barr, Alan P. "Christine de Pisan's Ditié de Jehanne d'Arc: A Feminist Exemplum for the Querelle des femmes." *Fifteenth Century Studies*. 14 (1988), 1–12.

Barstow, Anne Llewellyn. *Witchcraze: A New History of the European Witch Hunts*. New York: HarperOne, 1994.

Bartolini, Simone. *Sun and Symbols: The Zodiacs in the Basilica of San Miniato al Monte and in the Baptistry of San Giovanni in Florence*. Florence: Edizioni Polistampa, 2013.

Beaumont, Matthew. *Nightwalking: A Nocturnal History of London*. New York: Verso, 2015.

Behringer, Wolfgang. *Witches and Witch-Hunts: A Global History*. Cambridge, UK: Polity, 2004.

Bell, Matthew, ed. *The Essential Goethe*. Princeton, NJ: Princeton University Press, 2016.

Bever, Edward. "Popular Witch Beliefs and Magical Practices." *The Oxford Handbook of Early Modern Europe and Colonial America*. Brian P. Levack, ed. London: Oxford University Press, 2013.

Bodin, Jean. *De la Demonomanie des sorciers (On the Demon-mania of Witches)*. Trans. Randy A. Scott. Toronto: Centre for Reformation and Renaissance Studies, 1995.

Boguet, Henri. *An Examen of Witches*. Trans. E. A. Ashwin. London: Frederick Muller, 1971.

Boyer, Corinne. *Plants of the Devil*. Richmond Vista, CA: Three Hands Press, 2017.

Briggs, Robin. "Witchcraft and the Local Communities: The Rhine-Moselle Region." *The Oxford Handbook of Witchcraft in Early Modern Europe and Colonial America*. Brian P. Levack, ed. London: Oxford University Press, 2013.

Brown, Kathleen M. *Good Wives, Nasty Wenches & Anxious Patriarchs: Gender, Race, and Power in Colonial Virginia*. Chapel Hill: University of North Carolina Press, 1996.

Brucker, Gene, ed. *The Society of Renaissance Florence: A Documentary Study*. 1971. Toronto: University of Toronto Press, 2007.

Burr, George Lincoln. *Narratives of the New England Witchcraft Cases*. Mineola, NY: Dover Publications, 2002.

Butler, Jenny. "The Nearest Kin of the Moon: Irish Pagan Witchcraft, Magic(k), and the Celtic Twilight." *Magic and Witchery in the Modern West: Celebrating the Twentieth Anniversary of "The Triumph of the Moon."* London: Palgrave Macmillan, 2019.

Bynum, Caroline Walker. *Holy Feast and Holy Fast: The Religious Significance of Food to Medieval Women*. Los Angeles: University of California Press, 1988.

Callan, Maeve Brigid. *The Templars, the Witch, and the Wild Irish: Vengeance and Heresy in Medieval Ireland*. Ithaca, NY: Cornell University Press, 2015.

Callow, John. *Embracing the Darkness: A Cultural History of Witchcraft*. London: I.B. Tauris, 2018.

Camporesi, Piero. *Juice of Life: The Symbolic and Magic Significance of Blood.* Trans. Robert R. Barr. New York: Continuum, 1995.

Carr-Gomm, Philip, and Richard Heygate. *The Book of English Magic.* London: Hodder and Stoughton Ltd., 2009.

Cavendish, Richard. *The Black Arts: An Absorbing Account of Witchcraft, Demonology, Astrology, and other Mystical Practices throughout the Ages.* 1967. New York: Penguin Random House, 2017.

Chicago, Judy. *The Dinner Party: Restoring Women to History.* New York: The Monacelli Press, 2014.

Clark, Stuart. "Protestant Demonology: Sin, Superstition, and Society c. 1520–c. 1630." *Early Modern European Witchcraft: Centres and Peripheries.* Bengt Ankarloo and Gustav Henningsen, eds. London: Oxford University Press, 1993.

Collins, Derek. *Magic in the Ancient Greek World.* Hoboken, NJ: Wiley-Blackwell, 2008.

Cooper, John Michael, in *Mendelssohn, Goethe, and the Walpurgis Night.* Rochester, NY: University of Rochester Press, 2007.

Copenhaver, Brian, ed. *The Book of Magic: From Antiquity to the Enlightenment.* London: Penguin, 2015.

Corsi, Dina. *Diaboliche maledette e disperate: Le donne nei processi per stregoneria (secoli XIV-XVI).* Florence: Florence University Press, 2013.

Coverley, Merlin. *Psychogeography.* Harpenden, UK: Pocket Essentials, 2010.

Davies, Owen. *America Bewitched: The Story of Witchcraft after Salem.* London: Oxford University Press, 2013.

———. *Popular Magic: Cunning-folk in English History.* New York: Hambledon Continuum, 2007.

Davies, Owen, and Lisa Tallis. *Cunning Folk: An Introductory Bibliography.* London: The Folklore Society, 2005.

De Botton, Alain. *The Art of Travel.* London: Penguin, 2002.

Decker, Rainer. *Witchcraft and the Papacy*. Charlottesville: University of Virginia Press, 2008.

de Lancre, Pierre. *Tableau de L'inconstance Des Mauvais Anges Et Demons* (*On the Inconstancy of Witches*). Trans. Harriet Stone and Gerhild Scholz Williams. Ed. Gerhild Scholz Williams. Tempe: Arizona Center for Medieval and Renaissance Studies/Brepols, 2006.

Demos, John Putnam. *The Enemy Within: A Short History of Witch-Hunting*. New York: Penguin, 2008.

———. *Entertaining Satan: Witchcraft and the Culture of Early New England*. Oxford: Oxford University Press, 1982.

Dillinger, Johannes. "Germany—'the mother of the witches'." *The Routledge History of Witchcraft*. Johannes Dillinger, ed. London: Routledge, 2020.

Duni, Matteo. "Witchcraft and Witch Hunting in Late Medieval and Early Modern Italy." *The Routledge History of Witchcraft*. Johannes Dillinger, ed. London: Routledge, 2020.

Feinberg, Leslie. *Transgender Warriors: Making History from Joan of Arc to Dennis Rodman*. Boston: Beacon Press, 1997.

Ferree, Myra Marx. *Varieties of Feminism: German Gender Politics in Global Perspective*. Palo Alto, CA: Stanford University Press, 2012.

Ficino, Marsilio. *Three Books on Life: A Critical Edition and Translation with Introduction and Notes*. Carol V. Kaske and John R. Clark, eds. Binghamton, NY: Medieval and Renaissance Texts and Studies, 1989.

Field, Carol. *Celebrating Italy: Feasts, Festivals, and Foods*. New York: William Morrow & Co., 1990.

Gage, Matilda Joslyn. *Woman, Church and State*. Reprint. Watertown, MA: Persephone Press, 1980.

Games, Alison. *Witchcraft in Early North America*. Lanham, MD: Rowman & Littlefield, 2010.

Gibson, Marion. *Witchcraft: The Basics*. New York: Routledge, 2018.

Gibson, Marion. *Witchcraft Myths in American Culture*. Milton Park, Oxfordshire, UK: Routledge, 2007.

Goodare, Julian, ed. *The Scottish Witch Hunt in Context*. Manchester, UK: Manchester University Press, 2002.

Goodare, Julian; Lauren Martin; Joyce Miller; and Louise Yeoman. "The Survey of Scottish Witchcraft." *ed.ac.uk*. Archived January 2003. Accessed August 6, 2019.

Goodier, Christine. *1612: The Lancashire Witch Trials*. Lancaster, UK: Palatine Books, 2018.

Green, Monica H., trans. *The Trotula: A Medieval Compendium of Women's Medicine*. Philadelphia: University of Pennsylvania Press, 2001.

Grimassi, Raven. *Communing with the Ancestors: Your Spirit Guides, Bloodline Allies, and the Cycle of Reincarnation*. Newburyport, MA: Weiser Books, 2016.

Grossman, Pam. *Waking the Witch: Reflections on Women, Magic, and Power*. New York: Gallery Books, 2019.

Hastis, Thomas. *The Witches' Ointment: The Secret History of Psychedelic Magic*. Rochester, VT: Park Street Press, 2015.

Henderson, Lizanne. "'Detestable Slaves of the Devil': Changing Ideas about Witchcraft in Sixteenth-Century Scotland." *A History of Everyday Life in Medieval Scotland, 1000 to 1600. Vol. 1*. E. J. Cowan and Lizanne Henderson, eds. Edinburgh: Edinburgh University Press, 2011.

Herzig, Tamar. "Witches, Saints, and Heretics: Heinrich Kramer's Ties with Italian Women Mystics." *Magic, Ritual, and Witchcraft*, 1:1. (Summer 2006), pp. 24–55. Philadelphia: University of Pennsylvania Press, 2005.

Hester, Marianne. "Patriarchal Reconstruction and Witch Hunting." *Witchcraft in Early Modern Europe: Studies in Culture and Belief.* Jonathan Barry, Marianne Hester, Gareth Roberts, eds. Cambridge, UK: Cambridge University Press, 1996.

Hobbins, Daniel. *The Trial of Joan of Arc.* Cambridge, MA: Harvard University Press, 2007.

Horowitz, Mitch. *Occult America.* New York: Bantam, 2009.

Hudson Jr., Carson O. *Witchcraft in Colonial Virginia.* Charleston, SC: History Press, 2019.

Hults, Linda C. *The Witch as Muse: Art, Gender, and Power in Early Modern Europe.* Philadelphia: University of Pennsylvania Press, 2005.

Hutton, Ronald. *The Witch: A History of Fear, from Ancient Times to the Present.* New Haven, CT: Yale University Press, 2017.

———. *Witches, Druids, and King Arthur.* New York: Hambledon Continuum, 2006.

———. Ronald. "Witch Hunting in Celtic Societies." *Past & Present,* 212:1 (Aug. 2011), pp. 43–71.

Karlsen, Carol F. *The Devil in the Shape of a Woman: Witchcraft in Colonial New England.* New York: W. W. Norton, 1998.

Kennedy, Rick. *The First American Evangelical: A Short Life of Cotton Mather.* New York: Wm. B. Eerdmans Publishing Co., 2015.

Kieckhefer, Richard. *Magic in the Middle Ages.* Cambridge, UK: Cambridge University Press, 1990.

King, Margaret L. *Women of the Renaissance.* Chicago: University of Chicago Press, 1991.

Kramer, Heinrich, and Jacob Sprenger. *The Malleus Maleficarum.* ca. 1487. Montague Summers, trans. London: Arrow, 1971.

Larner, Christina. *Enemies of God: The Witch-Hunt in Scotland.* Baltimore, MD: Johns Hopkins University Press, 1981.

————."Was Witch-Hunting Woman-Hunting?" *New Society*, 58 (1981), pp. 11–12.

Lecouteux, Claude. *Demons and Spirits of the Land*. Rochester, VT: Inner Traditions, 1995.

Leeson, Peter T., and Jacob W. Russ. "The Witch Trials." *The Economic Journal*, 128:613 (Aug. 2018), pp. 2066–2105.

Levack, Brian P. *The Witchcraft Sourcebook*. London: Routledge, 2003.

————. *Witch Hunting in Scotland: Law, Politics and Religion*. London: Routledge, 2008.

Longstaffe, Moya. *Joan of Arc and "The Great Pity of the Land of France."* Gloucestershire, UK: Amberley Publishing, 2017.

Mather, Cotton. *The Wonders of the Invisible World*. 1693. Urbana, IL: Project Gutenberg. Retrieved December 15, 2019, from *gutenberg.org*

Michelet, Jules. *La Sorcière*. 1862; trans. A.R. Allinson as *Satanism and Witchcraft*. London: Tandem, 1965.

Molitor, Ulrich. *De lamiis et pythonicis mulieribus* (*On Female Witches and Seers*). Reutlingen, Germany: Johan Otmar, 1489.

Monter, William. "Witchcraft Trials in France." *The Oxford Handbook of Witchcraft in Early Modern Europe and Colonial America*. Brian P. Levack, ed. London: Oxford University Press, 2013.

Morgan, Robin. *The Burning Time*. Hoboken, NJ: Melville House Publishing, 2006.

Mormando, Franco. *The Preacher's Demons: Bernardino of Siena and the Social Underworld of Early Renaissance Italy*. Chicago: University of Chicago Press, 1999.

Nin, Anaïs. *The Diary of Anaïs Nin*, Vol. 7: 1966-1974. New York: Houghton Mifflin, 1981.

O'Donnell, James J. *Pagans: The End of Traditional Religion and the Rise of Christianity*. New York: HarperCollins, 2015.

Orion, Loretta. *It Were As Well to Please the Devil as Anger Him: Witchcraft in the Founding Days of East Hampton*. CreateSpace Independent Publishing Platform, 2018.

Ortega, Maria Helena Sanchez. "Sorcery and Eroticism in Love Magic." *Cultural Encounters: The Impact of the Inquisition in Spain and the New World*. Los Angeles: University of California Press, 1991.

Paule, Maxwell Teitel. *Canidia, Rome's First Witch*. London: Bloomsbury Academic, 2019.

Pearl, Jonathan L. *The Crime of Crimes: Demonology and Politics in France 1560–1620*. Waterloo, Ontario: Wilfrid Laurier University Press, 1999.

Pennick, Nigel. *Witchcraft & Secret Societies of Rural England*. Rochester, VT: Destiny Books, 2019.

Poltronieri, Morena, et al. *Tarot Travel Guide of Italy: History of a Mystery from the Renaissance*. Riola, Spain: Mutus Liber, 2015.

Praetorius, Johannes. *Blockes-Berges Verrichtung*. Leipzig: Scheiben, 1668.

Purkiss, Diane. *The Witch in History: Early Modern and Twentieth-Century Representations*. New York: Routledge, 1996.

Rankine, David, ed. *The Grimoire of Arthur Gauntlet: A 17th-Century London Cunning-man's Book of Charms, Conjurations and Prayers*. London: Avalonia, 2011.

Rediker, Marcus. *Between the Devil and the Deep Blue Sea: Merchant Seamen, Pirates and the Anglo-American Maritime World 1700–1750*. Cambridge, UK: Cambridge University Press, 1987.

Reynolds, Daniel P. *Postcards from Auschwitz: Holocaust Tourism and the Meaning of Remembrance*. New York: New York University Press, 2018.

Roach, Marilynn K. *Six Women of Salem: The Untold Story of the Accused and Their Accusers in the Salem Witch Trials*. Boston: Da Capo, 2013.

Roper, Lyndal. *Witch Craze: Terror and Fantasy in Baroque Germany.* New Haven, CT: Yale University Press, 2004.

———. *The Witch in the Western Imagination.* Charlottesville: University of Virginia Press, 2012.

Ross, Richard S., III. *Before Salem: Witch Hunting in the Connecticut River Valley, 1647–1663.* Jefferson, NC: McFarland & Company, Inc., Publishers, 2017.

Ruggiero, Guido. *Binding Passions: Tales of Magic, Marriage, and Power at the End of the Renaissance.* New York: Oxford University Press, 1993.

Russell, Jeffrey Burton. *Witchcraft in the Middle Ages.* Ithaca, NY: Cornell University Press, 1984.

Schiff, Stacy. "The Witches of Salem." *The New Yorker.* September 7, 2015.

———. *The Witches: Salem, 1692.* New York: Little, Brown & Co., 2015.

Scholz Williams, Gerhild. "Demonologies." *The Oxford Handbook of Early Modern Europe and Colonial America.* Brian P. Levack, ed. London: Oxford University Press, 2013.

Schulke, Daniel A. *Veneficium: Magic, Witchcraft and the Poison Path.* Richmond Vista, CA: Three Hands Press, 2017.

Schutte, Anne Jacobson. "'Saints' and 'Witches' in Early Modern Italy: Stepsisters or Strangers?" *Time, Space, and Women's Lives in Early Modern Europe.* Anne Jacobson et al., eds. Philadelphia: Penn State University Press, 2001.

Sharpe, James. "Witch Hunts in Britain." *The Routledge History of Witchcraft.* Johannes Dillinger, ed. London: Routledge, 2020.

Simon, Maryse. "Witch Hunts in France." *The Routledge History of Witchcraft.* Johannes Dillinger, ed. London: Routledge, 2020.

Snyder, Terri L. *Brabbling Women: Disorderly Speech and the Law in Early Virginia.* Ithaca, NY: Cornell University Press, 2014.

Soman, Alfred. "The Parlement of Paris and the Great Witch Hunt (1565-1640)." *The Sixteenth Century Journal.* 9:2 (Jul. 1978), 30–44.

Somerset, Anne. *The Affair of the Poisons: Murder, Infanticide, and Satanism at the Court of Louis XIV.* New York: St. Martins Press, 2014.

Sontag, Susan. *Regarding the Pain of Others.* New York: Farrar, Straus and Giroux, 2003.

Thurston, Robert W. "The Salem Witch Hunt." *The Routledge History of Witchcraft.* Johannes Dillinger, ed. London: Routledge, 2020.

Undset, Sigrid. *Catherine of Siena.* 1951. San Francisco: Ignatius Press, 2009.

van Luijk, Ruben. *Children of Lucifer: The Origins of Modern Religious Satanism.* London: Oxford University Press, 2016.

von Stuckrad, Kocku. *History of Western Astrology: From Earliest Times to the Present.* London: Equinox Publishing, 2007.

Waters, Thomas. *Cursed Britain: A History of Witchcraft and Black Magic in Modern Times.* New Haven, CT: Yale University Press, 2019.

Williams, Gerhild Scholz. *Ways of Knowing in Early Modern Germany: Johannes Praetorius as a Witness to His Time.* London: Routledge, 2006.

TO OUR READERS

Weiser Books, an imprint of Red Wheel/Weiser, publishes books across the entire spectrum of occult, esoteric, speculative, and New Age subjects. Our mission is to publish quality books that will make a difference in people's lives without advocating any one particular path or field of study. We value the integrity, originality, and depth of knowledge of our authors.

Our readers are our most important resource, and we appreciate your input, suggestions, and ideas about what you would like to see published.

Visit our website at *www.redwheelweiser.com* to learn about our upcoming books and free downloads, and be sure to go to *www.redwheelweiser.com/newsletter* to sign up for newsletters and exclusive offers.

You can also contact us at *info@rwwbooks.com* or at

Red Wheel/Weiser, LLC
65 Parker Street, Suite 7
Newburyport, MA 01950